Lesbians and Gay Men
as Foster Parents

Wendell Ricketts

National Child Welfare Resource Center
Center for Child and Family Policy
Edmund S. Muskie Institute of Public Affairs
University of Southern Maine

1991

This volume is dedicated to the memory of Doug Warner, whose ability to bridge the distance between the world of adults and the world of children was a marvel to behold, and whose joy in his adopted nieces and nephews embodied the highest meaning of family.

Flamingoes and Bears

Flamingoes and bears
meet secretly
on odd street corners.
Horses and chickens
elephants and geese
looked shocked and appalled.

Ostriches don't look at all.

Bear and flamingo
ignore greedy gazes
from disgruntled parents
and frightened sly weasels
who hiss
as the couple
strolls by.

Chance brought them here
from forest and sea,
but science won't agree
where
bears and flamingoes
learned how simple
building a nest
in a den can be.

Now flamingo and bear
sleep forever entwined
in all sorts of climes
be it rainy or snowy or sunny,
happy to know
there's room in this world
for a bear who likes palm trees

and a bird who loves honey.

— Jewelle L. Gomez

"Flamingoes and Bears" originally appeared in Jewelle Gomez's book of poems of the same name, published by Grace Publications, Jersey City, New Jersey in 1986. It is used by permission of the author.

Acknowledgements

The author is deeply indebted to Donna Hitchens, Roberta Achtenberg, and Kevin Cathcart for their unfailingly generous gifts of time, information, and advice. In addition, I would like to thank Helaine Hornby and Loren Coleman of the National Child Welfare Resource Center for Management and Administration for their faith in this project and, in particular, for their patience and many courtesies. Finally, I will always be grateful to the many men, women, and young people who unselfishly shared with me their experiences of family, and in so doing profoundly shaped my thinking.

CHAPTER ONE

Why Deal With This Issue?

All across the country, tens of thousands of lesbians and gay men are already providing homes for many of America's foster children. Some of these men and women are not known as gay or lesbian to the agencies that have placed children with them — but many others are known openly. In some cases, agencies recognize that foster-parent recruitment chronically falls far below the need for foster homes, and staff and social workers look the other way as a "probably" gay or lesbian home is licensed. Ricketts and Achtenberg, for example, recorded this frank comment from the director of a foster home program in Washington, D.C.:

> We've always had pairs of women providing foster care. In some instances, they have not been related. And of course, that always raises questions in some people's minds. But as far as we were concerned, they were two friends who lived together and wanted to do this together. I would assume that some of the people who apply to be foster parents might be gay. But if they are, we don't know about it.[1]

At times, individuals at different levels of an agency may be "out of synch" with one another regarding the placement of children with lesbian or gay foster parents. The social worker who visits and studies a home, for example, may have very pragmatic reasons for finding the placement to be acceptable;

---

[1] Ricketts, W. & Achtenberg, R. A. (1990). Adoption and foster parenting for lesbians and gay men: Creating new traditions in family. *Marriage and Family Review*, 14(3/4), 83-118, p. 84.

but an agency administrator may disfavor the same home because of considerations ranging from the potential for negative publicity to the perceived political climate within the agency itself.

At the other end of the spectrum are cities like San Francisco, where the Foster Home Program of the county Department of Social Services employs a liaison to the lesbian and gay community. Alternately, state or county personnel may work alongside private agencies such as Los Angeles's Triangle Project, an organization dedicated to the recruitment and training of gay and lesbian foster parents for Southern California's burgeoning population of runaways and street kids.[2]

On several occasions during recent years, media have focused their attention on the "problem" of homosexual foster parenting. Perhaps the most widely publicized case began in 1985 and involved two young children placed in, then suddenly removed from, the licensed foster home of a Boston, Massachusetts gay couple, Donald Babets and David Jean.

Almost immediately, the Babets and Jean case erupted into heated debate, and the Massachusetts Department of Social Services was embroiled in controversy. Governor Michael Dukakis was pressured to take a stand on lesbian and gay foster parenting during an election year and, shortly after the children were removed, the DSS promulgated new regulations that effectively prohibited all future foster placements with lesbians or gay men.

In the aftermath, the efforts of the DSS to deal with the placement, its "exposure," and the resulting controversy were widely evaluated and criticized in the media, within agencies, in the political arena, and in private. Ultimately, the Babets and Jean case resulted in a lawsuit against Governor Dukakis and the Commonwealth of Massachusetts. That litigation was finally settled, and the ban reversed, in April, 1990. (The Babets and Jean case is described in detail in Chapter Five.)

---

[2]   Ricketts, W. (1987, July 21). Triangle Project: Placing homeless gay youths with supportive gay parents. *The Advocate* (Advocate West), 12-14.

Because it could be repeated anywhere in the country, the Massachusetts experience is instructive. With the shortage of good foster homes and the growing willingness of gay men and lesbians to be open about their lives, children's service agencies must address the issue of placing children with homosexuals, must educate their personnel regarding questions and concerns presented by lesbian and gay parenting, and must set policies they are willing and able to defend. Without such resolutions, media controversies and public battles can demoralize an agency's staff and waste time and resources that are better spent in the service of children.

Foster Parent Recruitment And The Changing Family

There is growing recognition that the foster-parent pool is dwindling and that foster parent recruitment efforts are not overwhelmingly successful. At the same time, however, the population of children who must be placed in foster care is on the rise. A study released by the House of Representatives Select Committee on Children, Youth and Families indicated that the number of children in foster care rose 23 percent between 1985 and 1988, and estimated that more than 840,000 children would be in foster care by 1995.[3]

The report confirmed the findings of other experts, such as Smith and Gutheil[4], who attribute the growth in out-of-home placements to such factors as increased poverty and homelessness, drug abuse and AIDS, and a rising number of pregnant teenagers with little or no family support. Child welfare experts who testified at Congressional hearings in 1987 added another factor to the list: a 55 percent increase between 1981 and 1985 in reports of

---

[3]   "Alarming" Congressional report: Many more children not living at home. (1989, December 12). *San Francisco Chronicle*, A-14.

[4]   Smith, E. P. & Gutheil, R. H. (1988). Successful foster parent recruiting: A voluntary agency effort. *Child Welfare, 67*(2), 137-146.

child abuse or neglect.[5] Others blame what is perhaps a more politically controversial influence — cuts in federal and state human-services budgets throughout the 80s.

As one case in point, the State of California, whose foster care system has been seriously overburdened for years, is now being forced to house children for up to a year in shelters that are meant to provide only short-term care.[6] Jeannette Dunckel, a spokesperson for the Children's Research Institute, which studies California's foster care system, noted that

> some of the sickest and [most] emotionally deprived children are in shelters rather than in foster homes. "They're not getting the kind of nurturing they need because they're lingering for such a long time in shelter care."[7]

In the city of San Francisco, the crises in foster care are likewise typical of those confronting most American cities today: poverty, disease, the crack-cocaine epidemic, and increased reporting of child abuse have sent children "cascading" into the foster care system.[8] In addition, the critical need for foster homes has led to numerous out-of-county placements — a situation that makes visitation by and reunification with families of origin even more difficult. In 1989, in fact, San Francisco reunited only 125 of the 2,750 children placed in foster care that year.

Finally, the growing demands of the caseload have forced social workers to be responsible for one-third or more cases than

5   House Select Committee on Children, Youth and Families. (1987, April 22). Hearings before the House of Representatives, 100th Congress, 1st Session. *Continuing crisis in foster care: Issues and problems.* Washington, DC: U. S. Government Printing Office.

6   Stewart. P. (1989, December 5). Groups report big shortage of foster care. *San Francisco Chronicle*, A-4.

7   *Ibid.*

8   Seligman, K. (1990, April 13). SF system struggling to serve more needy kids. San Francisco *Chronicle*, A-1, A-22, p.A-1.

they can reasonably oversee. As a result, some children "go for months, even years without a visit from their social workers."[9] Comparable statistics and similar conditions are the rule in urban areas throughout the United States.

Researchers Smith and Gutheil[10] and Moore, Granpre and Scoll,[11] for example, report that a diminishing number of foster parents forced their agencies (located in New York City and Hennepin County, Minnesota, respectively) to take unprecedented measures to recruit additional foster parents. These efforts included paying existing foster parents to recruit new homes[12] and employing "Madison Avenue" market research techniques in an effort to identify outreach and recruitment strategies that were effective with target groups of potential foster parents.[13]

Finally, there is widespread acknowledgement on the part of family experts that families in America are undergoing rapid, wide-scale change. By 1986, for example, groups of married couples with children — the traditional "nuclear" family — made up only 27.8 percent of all family households in America.[14]

During the 1980s, in fact, the children of divorced, separated, or never-married parents were becoming a commonplace feature in America's public schools, playgroups, and daycare centers. Census data tell us that single-parent families grew from 12.8 percent of family groups in 1970 to 26.3 percent in 1986 — a figure that represents nearly nine million households.[15] Experts anticipate, moreover, that 60 percent of all children born in the 1980s

---

9   *Ibid.*, p. A-22.

10   Smith & Gutheil, *supra.*

11   Moore, B., Granpre, M. & Scoll, B. (1988). Foster home recruitment: A market research approach to attracting and licensing applicants. *Child Welfare, 67*(2), 147-160.

12   Smith & Gutheil, *supra.*

13   Moore, et al., *supra.*

14   U.S. Bureau of the Census. (1987). *The Statistical Abstract of the United States: 1988* (108th ed.). Washington, D.C.: Government Printing Office.

15   *Ibid.*

will live for some period with only one of their parents.[16] Step-families, too, are growing rapidly, and it is currently estimated that at least one child in every four will live with a step-parent by age 16.[17]

Nearly a decade ago, Alvin Toffler assessed changing family trends in *The Third Wave* and noted:

> If we define the nuclear family as a working hus-band, housekeeping wife, and two children, and ask how many Americans actually still live in this type of family, the answer is astonishing: 7 percent of the total United States population.... Even if we broaden our definition to include families in which both spouses work or in which there are fewer or more than two children, we find the vast majority — as many as two thirds to three quarters of the population — living *outside* the nuclear situation. Moreover, all the evidence suggests that nuclear households (however we choose to define them) are still shrinking in number as other family forms rapidly multiply.[18]

By the end of the 1980s, such "other family forms" were, indeed, proliferating. In November, 1989, *Newsweek* magazine documented these changes in a special issues entitled *The 21st Century Family* and noted, in its cover story:

> The American family does not exist. Rather, we are creating many American families, of diverse styles and shapes. In unprecedented numbers, our families are unlike: We have fathers working while mothers keep house; fathers and mothers both working away from home; single parents;

---

[16]   Measures of Change. (1989, December 25 - 1990, January 1). *U.S. News and World Report*, 66-67.

[17]   *Ibid.*

[18]   Toffler, A. (1980). *The third wave.* NY: Doubleday, pp.227-228.

second marriages bringing children together from unrelated backgrounds; childless couples; unmarried couples, with and without children; gay and lesbian parents. We are living through a period of historic change in American family life.[19]

At the same time, estimates of the number of children who live in lesbian- or gay-parented families — including children conceived in heterosexual marriages — range from 1.5 million[20] to as high as 14 million.[21] In urban centers such as San Francisco, Boston, New York, and elsewhere, a growing number of lesbians and gay men are becoming parents through adoption, artificial insemination, or group- and co-parenting with other lesbians or gay men. Some of these family constellations include gay men and lesbians who legally marry one another, lesbians who co-parent with heterosexual men, and two or more sets of same-sex couples who share parenting responsibilities for children to whom they may or may not be biologically related.[22]

Given all these facts, it is safe to conclude that the Ozzie-and-Harriet-type home — whether as a norm of American life or as an ideal for foster placements — will be harder and harder to find. Indeed, Toni Oliver of the National Center for Neighborhood Enterprise in Washington D.C., criticized what she called "American Dream Family" criteria that effectively rule out large numbers of potential foster parents. Noting that only 13 percent of foster homes actually meet "American Dream" criteria, Oliver noted,

[19]   Footlick, J. K. (1990, Winter/Spring). What happened to the family? *Newsweek* (Special Issue), 14-18+, p. 15.

[20]   Hunter, N. & Polikoff, N. (1976). Custody rights of lesbian mothers: Legal theory and litigation strategy. *Buffalo Law Review, 25,* 691-733, p. 691.

[21]   Coming to terms with gay parents. (1984, April 3). *USA Today,* 1. *See* also Bozett, F. W. (1988). Social control of identity by children of gay fathers. *Western Journal of Nursing Research,* 10(5), 550-565; and O'Toole, M. T. (1989). Gay parenting: Myths and realities. *Pace Law Review,* 9, 129-164.

[22]   Ghent, Janet Silver. (1990, June 20). New spin on the American family. *Oakland Tribune,* D-1, D-2.

"[Such] attitudes contribute largely to children being locked out and lost in the child welfare system."[23]

Family experts, as a result, have begun calling for flexibility in concepts of family — are suggesting, that is, that legislators, courts, human services experts, and other policy-makers adopt definitions of family that simply acknowledge the ways in which people actually live. A growing number of cities, in fact, have appointed committees to study changes in family demographics and to suggest guidelines for family policy in the 1990s.

In 1988, for example, the City of Los Angeles appointed a Task Force on Family Diversity to study family groupings in Los Angeles's communities and to make a series of recommendations to the City's various human services agencies. In its 125-page final report, the Task Force noted:

> Recognizing human diversity is very different from making judgments about it. [We need not] engage in the endless academic debate over the relative merits of different lifestyles, personalities, relationships, or types of family structures. Instead, [we can] focus on the importance of learning to live and work together constructively to solve problems. In a world that mass communications and close urban living have made so small, alienating judgments do not better the quality of life for anyone.
>
> ...
>
> The recognition of the value of diversity is deeply rooted in our nation's history and philosophical origins. Pluralism has created for us a strong society, and respect for human diversity is a prerequisite to tapping the full potential of our vast reservoir of human talent.[24]

---

[23] House Select Committee, *supra*, p. 146.

[24] City of Los Angeles Task Force on Family Diversity. (1988). *Final Report: Strengthening Families — A Model for Community Action*. Los Angeles, CA: Author, p. vi.

Indeed, to the extent that families "maintain the physical health and safety of [their] members; help shape a belief system of goals and values; teach social skills[;] and create a place for recuperation from external stresses,"[25] a family may be constellated in a variety of ways beyond the "one mommy/one daddy" model. As American University Law Professor Nancy Polikoff noted,

> If the family is the "basic unit of society" because it is the unit within which children are reared, lesbian-mother [and gay-father] families simply add to the number of "basic units of society."[26]

Lesbian and Gay Foster Parents — An Untapped Resource?

Ensuring the care and protection of its foster children is surely one of America's most demanding child welfare problems. In meeting that challenge, social service agencies may find advantages in considering lesbians and gay men as potential foster parents.

Particularly in urban settings with organized gay and lesbian communities, for example, prospective foster parents could be drawn from a comparatively well-employed and well-educated population whose disposable income may also be higher than average. Such individuals represent a largely untapped resource in the effort to meet the needs of America's foster children.

Although lesbian and gay foster parenting remains controversial, it is not untested. We have already noted the San Francisco and Los Angeles experiences, where open lesbian and gay foster parent homes are currently in place — a situation that has been duplicated in Washington, D.C., Minneapolis, New York, and a

---

25 Footlick, *supra*, p. 18.

26 Polikoff, N. D. (1990, February). This child does have two mothers: Redefining parenthood to meet the needs of children in lesbian-mother and other nontraditional families. *Georgetown Law Journal, 78*(3), 459-575.

number of other American cities. In fact, open gay and lesbian foster homes have been in existence since the early- to mid-70s.[27]

More recently, in addition, some urban agencies have begun to identify the lesbian and gay community as a source from which to recruit foster parents for HIV-infected babies.[28] Existing lesbian and gay families, then, including foster families, can provide essential information about lesbian and gay parenting, and can calm the fears that often surround this emerging family form. (See also Chapter Four and Appendix B on lesbian and gay parenting.)

It is important to remember, moreover, that when open lesbians and gay men have succeeded in becoming foster parents, they have done so only after being thoroughly and rigorously evaluated. In most cases, in fact, as Ricketts and Achtenberg report, lesbians and gay men who apply to become foster parents are investigated even more extensively than other applicants.[29] Those who are licensed, then, have truly had to "measure up." In fact, given agencies' typical resistance to the idea of approving a gay or lesbian home,

> [M]any of the gay men and lesbians who success-
> fully traverse the foster care system bring with
> them special skills, training, resources, and stabil-
> ity. Frequently, those who succeed in being li-
> censed have, in addition to other abilities, a
> knowledge of how to work within bureaucracies
> that serves them well in social service delivery
> systems.[30]

---

[27] *See*, e.g., Agency reveals kids placed with gay couples. (1973, August 15). *The Advocate*, #118, 2 [Chicago, IL]; CA gay foster homes approved. (1976, June 30). *The Advocate*, #193, 11; Franks, L. (1974, May 30). Teens who have gay 'parents.' *San Francisco Chronicle*, 22 [New York City]; and Judge places gay teenage boy in lesbian foster parents' home. (1974, May 22). *The Advocate*, #138, 8 [Philadelphia, PA].

[28] Gurdin, P. & Anderson, G. R. (1988). Quality care for ill children: AIDS-specialized foster family homes. *Child Welfare, 66*(4), 291-302.

[29] Ricketts, W. & Achtenberg, R. A. (1987). The adoptive and foster gay and lesbian parent. In F. W. Bozett (Ed.), *Gay and lesbian parents* (pp. 89-111). New York: Praeger Press.

[30] Ricketts & Achtenberg, 1990, *supra*, p. 100.

When controversy arises over a lesbian or gay placement, as sometimes happens, it is generally due to fears about "exposing" children to a lesbian or gay "lifestyle," or about influencing the sexual development of the child; or to a belief that homosexuality should automatically disqualify a potential foster parent — not because a particular gay man or lesbian has, through actions or omissions, shown him- or herself to be an unsuitable foster parent.

In 1988, for example, a lesbian couple in Alameda County, California began a lengthy legal battle that resulted in their being jointly licensed as foster parents for — and later in their joint adoption of — a baby boy with AIDS. Apart from being lesbians, ironically, the women were more "traditional" in their family unit than many married heterosexual foster parents: Millie Jessen worked as a computer programmer for a large for-profit corporation and Sue Pavlik stayed home as a full-time homemaker.

Jessen and Pavlik took baby Eric into their home as a foster child when he was just five weeks old. Not long after, they decided they wanted to adopt him. By Eric's second birthday, however, the Alameda County Department of Social Services was still refusing to approve the adoption, despite the fact that Eric's health had improved dramatically in Jessen and Pavlik's care and that Eric's biological father had enthusiastically consented to the adoption. In the end, a court order was required to make the adoption final.

Millie, Sue, and Eric's story received widespread media attention from Honolulu to New York[31] (as well as from several European television stations). Among other things, the publicity added to a growing recognition of the potential benefits of lesbian and gay foster and adoptive homes. In addition, since the Alameda County DSS never suggested that Jessen and Pavlik

---

[31]   California's adoption policy is criticized. (1989, November 16). *New York Times*, n.p.; Policy against adoption by unmarrieds is assailed. (1989, November 19). *Honolulu Star-Bulletin & Advertiser*, E-12.

were anything but loving and exceptionally skillful parents, the coverage also called into question the rationality of blanket prohibitions against lesbian and gay foster or adoptive parents.

Must There Be A Separate Policy for Lesbians and Gay Men?

In Boston, Massachusetts in 1985, on the other hand, the debate over foster care policy took quite a different turn. When the story of the Babets and Jean placement first broke in the Boston *Globe* (see Chapter Five), opponents of the placement immediately took the offensive, asking "Why doesn't the Commonwealth already have a policy regarding homosexual foster parents?" What the question actually meant, of course, was why was there no policy *prohibiting* the placement of children with gay men and lesbians. As Ricketts and Achtenberg commented,

> Like most states, it was true, Massachusetts' foster care policy made no specific mention of gay or lesbian applicants. But Governor Dukakis and the Massachusetts DSS blindly accepted the *Globe's* premise — that not having a specific policy was evidence of negligence or indifference on their parts.[32]

To a large degree, the "separate policy" issue can be evaluated in light of other commitments to non-discrimination that an agency may already have made. For example, does the agency have a separate policy governing Black, Asian, or Hispanic foster parent applicants? Are special standards applied to prospective foster parents who are wealthy vs. poor, highly vs. poorly educated, or young vs. old? Is there a unique policy regarding married foster parent applicants if the members of the couple are of different races or religions? Are single male applicants evaluated according to different protocols than single females?

---

[32] Ricketts & Achtenberg, 1987, *supra*, p. 101.

The answer to these questions is generally "no" because virtually every child-placing service is required to refrain from discriminating against prospective foster parents on the basis of sex, age, race, marital status, and other similar factors. If an agency decides to expand its recruiting procedures to include lesbians and gay men, or officially to recognize the gay men and lesbians already within its foster parent pool, there is no reason that sexual orientation cannot be incorporated into existing equal-treatment guidelines.

But do any individuals or groups have an inherent right to be foster parents? Because foster parenting is a government-created and government-regulated activity — and is a function that the foster parent shares with the state — courts have routinely held that no "right" to become a foster parent exists. The constitutionally protected "liberty interest" inherent in biological parenting, that is, has not been extended to the relationships a foster parent may form with a foster child.

Children in the care of the state, however, do have certain legal rights, including the right to expect that their best interests will be served by child-placing agencies. That said, it seems likely that most child welfare organizations will want to undertake a sober assessment of the ways in which foster children may be affected if placements with available, qualified lesbian and gay foster parents are limited or banned.

What lesbian and gay activists (and others who support lesbian and gay foster parenting) have called for, in any case, is neither the "right" to be foster parents nor the dilution of child welfare criteria. Rather, advocates have asked, first, that prospective lesbian and gay foster parents be evaluated against the same standards and guidelines that all other potential foster parents face. In short, they have asserted the right of lesbians and gay men not to be foster parents, but to be considered fairly, and to be approved or rejected on the same bases as are all other applicants.

Second, proponents of lesbian and gay foster parenting have asked that the "best-interests-of-the-child" standard be applied consistently, without a *priori* rejection of qualified gays and lesbians on the basis of inaccurate stereotypes and irrational fears.

Personal Values vs. Public Stands

Obviously, agency administrators may already possess firm beliefs regarding whether children should be placed with lesbian or gay foster parents. They are aware, moreover, that an agency's policy affects many others who are involved, directly or indirectly, in the issue of gay and lesbian foster parenting. These include:

People directly affected by the policy, such as

- Gay men and lesbians who may wish to take foster children into their homes or to adopt children;

- Relatives and close friends of lesbians and gay men;

- Children who may or may not be placed in lesbian or gay homes;

- Birthparents, other relatives, and close family friends of children in need of foster home placement;

- The social worker assigned to the case; and

- Other social workers, administrators, and personnel at other social services agencies involved in the placement.

People indirectly affected by the policy, including organized "watchdog" groups who monitor public policy to ensure that their point of view is heard and who advocate particular political positions. Some of these might be:

- Religious groups that are vehemently anti-homosexual;

- Secular groups that take an anti-homosexual stance;

- Civil rights groups that defend lesbian and gay rights;

- Lesbian and gay political action groups.

Some of an agency's considerations might include these:

1. An agency will be profoundly affected by whatever policy it chooses. What will happen to the agency and its personnel if its policy regarding gay and lesbian foster parents is challenged? If the policy is exposed negatively in the media or is the subject of angry meetings, are agency administrators prepared to defend it? Is there enough support both inside and outside of the agency to ride out a potential controversy?

2. What if the agency must defend its policy? Administrators should consider very carefully the reasons for setting policy and, in particular, must:

a) *Educate and sensitize agency personnel* to issues related to children and homosexuality, sexual orientation development, and lesbian and gay foster parenting; *make use of coalitions* with professional child welfare associations, child-serving groups, community-based organizations, and supportive politicians; and *develop strategies* for dealing with media. A thoughtful, affirmative strategy beforehand is always preferable to a defensive reaction after the fact.

b) *Understand and anticipate arguments* for the other side. If an administrator is unaware of opposing arguments before a confrontation begins, he or she will be thrown off guard by issues and positions for which no response has been developed.

c) *Respect arguments* for the other side. If an administrator takes the attitude that those who oppose an agency's policy are immoral, bigoted, or insensitive, she or he will create barriers to any meeting of the minds that might take place. Rather than provide a measure of reassurance to all sides about standards for the placement of children, about the evaluation of potential foster parents, and about the agency's commitment to protecting the best interests of children, an adversarial administrator will only provoke further entrenchment and distrust. It is important to recognize, for example, that opponents of an open policy toward qualified lesbian and gay foster parents are genuinely afraid of losing something they consider to be crucial.

At the same time, however, certain kinds of unfounded beliefs and intractable prejudices must give way when tested against standards of justice and rationality. As discussed in Chapter Four, concerns about child molestation by homosexuals and about psychological and emotional harm to children who live with lesbians or gay men have been answered by social science research. A certain number of people, however, will refuse to give up their beliefs in homosexual "perversion, sickness, and immorality" no matter what information they are given.

Gordon Allport, in his monumental exploration of prejudice and of remedial efforts to change it, noted:

> It always has been thought that planting right ideas in the mind would engender right behavior.... But the [individual's] readiness to learn facts, it is now pretty well agreed, depends upon the state of his attitudes. Information seldom sticks unless mixed with attitudinal glue.[33]

What Allport's work suggests is that some individuals will not easily relinquish beliefs about homosexuality that they hold to be obviously true or essential to a personal sense of continuity and social order. Indeed, many so-called "truths" about lesbians and gay men are of this self-evident variety. Such beliefs are often expressed through phrases such as "Everyone knows that...." or "Common sense dictates that....".

These are precisely the kinds of arguments that have, for centuries, been used to oppress women ("Common sense tells us that a woman can't do a man's work"), Blacks ("Everyone knows that black people prefer their own kind and don't really want to mix with whites"), the poor ("We don't need a study to know that if people really wanted to work, they'd go get jobs"), and many other disenfranchised groups in American society.

---

[33] Allport, G. W. (1958). *The nature of prejudice* (abridged). Garden City, NY: Doubleday, p. 451. (Original work published 1954). *See*, also, Chapters 29 to 31, *passim*.

It is not uncommon for prejudice to be masked by "easy answers" like these, but when it comes to an issue as important as the welfare of children, we cannot afford to stop there. Before personal values become public policy — and carry with them the sanction of government — it is essential to ask *why* and *how*, and to find out what kinds of solid, reliable information exist to support a particular belief or position.

Lesbians and Gay Men as Foster Parents contains some of this information, and it points the reader toward a wide variety of additional resources. This manual is dedicated to all men and women who care deeply about families and about the welfare of America's children.

CHAPTER TWO

Examining Anti-Homosexual Attitudes and the Heterosexual Bias

An Overview of the Lesbian and Gay Rights Movement

In general, lesbians and gay men have begun to live openly only within the last thirty to forty years. Historian Alan Berube documents the growth of a homosexual "underground" during and after World War II, partly as a result of the war-time influx into many American cities of young, unmarried soldiers of both sexes.[34] The first more-or-less public homosexual organizations began to flourish in those post-war years, including the Daughters of Bilitis and the Mattachine Society. Other historians, however, note that homosexual emancipation groups existed in Germany, England, and even the United States as early as the latter part of the nineteenth century.[35]

In 1948 and 1953, the Institute for Sex Research at Indiana University, under the direction of Dr. Alfred C. Kinsey, issued its famous reports on the sex lives of American men and women.[36]

---

[34]   Berube, A. (1989). Marching to a different drummer: Lesbian and gay GIs in World War II. In M. B. Duberman, M. Vicinus, & G. Chauncey, Jr. (Eds.), *Hidden from history: Reclaiming the gay and lesbian past* (pp. 383-394). NY: New American Library. *See* also Berube's *Coming out under fire: The history of gay men and women in World War Two.* NY: The Free Press (Macmillan), 1990.

[35]   Lauritsen, J. & Thorstad, D. (1974). *The early homosexual rights movement (1864-1935).* NY: Times Change Press.

[36]   Kinsey, A. C., Pomeroy, W. B., & Martin, C. E. (1948). *Sexual behavior in the human male.* Philadelphia, PA: W. B. Saunders Company; Kinsey, A. C., Pomeroy, W. B., Martin, C. E., & Gebhard, P. H. (1953). *Sexual behavior in the human female.* Philadelphia, PA: W. B. Saunders Company.

The Institute's two landmark volumes were the result of the first (and, to date, only) wide-scale survey of the sexual behavior of tens of thousands of Americans. Among their many detailed and controversial findings, the Kinsey group offered evidence that homosexual behavior was anything but rare. Of Kinsey's male respondents, for example, well over one-third had participated in at least one same-sex experience during adulthood, and 10 percent were more-or-less exclusively homosexual between adolescence and old age. The comparable figures for women were slightly lower.

Although the Kinsey findings were roundly attacked by those who refused to believe that homosexuals constituted any but the tiniest of minorities, the Reports' methodology has ultimately proven to be sound. As a result, the work of Kinsey and his colleagues is still routinely consulted as an authority on human sexual behavior. In the long term, the Kinsey Reports helped set the stage for the beginning of a reconsideration of homosexuality in American society.

In 1954, on the other side of the Atlantic, the British government commissioned the Wolfenden Committee

> to consider the law and practice relating to homo-
> sexual offenses and the treatment of persons con-
> victed of such offenses by the courts;... and to
> report what changes, if any, are in our opinion
> desirable.[37]

Three years later, the Committee published its recommendations, including, among other things, the suggestion that all laws prohibiting private sexual behavior of any kind between consenting adults be struck down.

Despite the considerable changes that took place in the 1950s and 1960s, and the new information about human sexuality that was beginning to be available in America and elsewhere, homo-

---

[37] *The Wolfenden report: Report of the Departmental Committee on Homosexual Offenses and Prostitution.* (1964). NY: Lancer Books. (Original work published 1957), p. 15.

sexuals continued to be persecuted socially and legally during those years. On June 27, 1969, a routine bar raid at The Stonewall Inn, a working-class gay bar in New York's Greenwich Village, proved to be the catalyst for the modern gay rights movement. For the first time, homosexuals gathered at The Stonewall fought back en masse against police harassment. Days of intermittent rioting followed.

In the wake of the civil disobedience and street activism that accompanied the Stonewall uprising, the Gay Liberation Front (GLF) was founded. GLF, Homosexuals Intransigent, the Gay Activist Alliance, the Committee for Homosexual Freedom, and others were among the many open, even militant gay organizations that drew strength from the growing refusal of gay men, lesbians, and other members of society's sexual "fringe" to remain cowed and closeted. They paved the way for the literally hundreds of political, legal, social, and advocacy organizations that have emerged in the years since.[38]

Ultimately, in fact, lesbians and gay men linked their cause to the social protest and liberation ethic that swept America in the 1960s and 1970s and, by 1979, 39 American cities and counties had enacted ordinances banning discrimination against gay men and lesbians in such areas as housing and employment.[39] There were other signs of progress as well — but there were also indications of a growing backlash. Anita Bryant's 1977 "Save Our Children" campaign, for example, energized successful efforts to repeal anti-discrimination laws in several cities.

By 1980, the "New Right" swept Ronald Reagan and scores of other "traditional values" candidates into offices all across the nation, and by 1981, a new disease was beginning to terrify the lesbian and gay community. One year later, medical researchers would name the disease "AIDS." Since then, lesbian and gay activists have been occupied with caring for their afflicted friends

---

[38] On the early years of gay liberation, *see*, e.g., Teal, D. (1971). *The gay militants*. NY: Stein and Day.

[39] Masters, W. H. & Johnson, V. E. (1979). *Homosexuality in perspective*. Boston: Little, Brown, p. 347.

and loved ones and with attempts to secure adequate funding for AIDS research, health services, and prevention efforts.

The "movement," however, has not gone dormant. As lesbians and gay men continue their struggle for dignity and respect, they have been joined by many friends, including the numerous organizations that have officially declared their support for the civil rights of lesbian and gay people (such as the American Medical Association, the American Bar Association, the American Association for the Advancement of Science, the American Public Health Association, the American Anthropological Association, the American Federation of Teachers, the AFL-CIO, the American Personnel and Guidance Association, and the American Civil Liberties Union).

In addition, lesbians and gay men continue to win significant legal battles in such areas as employment, child custody, housing, partners' rights, and even the military,[40] and to insist on acceptance within their families, communities, churches, and in society as a whole. For many gay men and lesbians, however, one of the most important phases of the struggle for justice into the 1990s is obtaining recognition of their family partnerships and of their relationships with the children in their lives.

Homophobia and the Heterosexual Bias

Despite political, social, and legal advances by lesbians and gay men, however, a large number of Americans continue to believe that homosexuals deserve to be treated as second-class citizens — or worse. Social scientists call this phenomenon "homophobia" (loosely defined both as the fear of homosexuals or of homosexuality *and* as the entire domain of anti-gay attitudes). Studies show that homophobia is commonly associated with other characteristics such as religious orthodoxy and high levels of

---

[40]   *See,* e.g., Leonard, A. S. (1990, July 2). Gay/lesbian rights: Report from the legal front. *The Nation,* 12-15.

authoritarianism, as well as with racism, support for "traditional," restrictive sex roles, and other forms of social prejudice.[41]

Homophobia and heterosexual bias are expressed in many ways. Homosexuals are made the butt of vicious jokes by popular comedians such as Eddie Murphy and Andrew Dice Clay. They are caricatured in popular movies and on television, and are increasingly the victims of physical violence and homicide. They are banned from the military and most ministries, and are commonly denied jobs and housing. Even today, heterosexually married lesbians and gay men often lose custody of their biological children when those marriages break up.

What is more, there are almost no legal protections for the relationships formed by gay men and lesbians. Gay and lesbian family partners are commonly denied the material advantages of heterosexual marriages (such as tax benefits, various kinds of "family memberships," single-policy insurance coverage of homes they own jointly, discounts on auto insurance and vacation packages, and community property and inheritance rights). They often find, moreover, that they are barred from caring for — or even visiting — their ill or incapacitated partners.[42]

---

[41] *See,* e.g., Herek, G. M. (1984). Beyond "homophobia": A social psychological perspective on attitudes toward lesbians and gay men. *Journal of Homosexuality, 10*(1/2), 1-21, pp. 6-7; Larsen, K. S., Cate, R. & Reed, M. (1983). Antiblack attitudes, religious orthodoxy, permissiveness, and sexual information. *Journal of Sex Research, 19*(2), 105-118; and Smith, K. T. (1971). Homophobia: A tentative personality profile. *Psychological Reports, 29*, 1091-1094.

[42] *See,* e.g., Thompson, K. & Andrzejewski, J. (1988). *Why can't Sharon Kowalski come home?* San Francisco: Spinsters/Aunt Lute. Sharon Kowalski and Karen Thompson were family partners in Minnesota when Sharon was seriously brain injured and paralyzed in a car accident. For several years after, Sharon's family denied Karen all contact with their daughter. Karen has waged an ongoing legal battle for the right to care for Sharon and, in the process, has focused attention on the lack of protection afforded lesbian and gay domestic partners. Karen and Sharon were reunited by court order in late 1989.

[43] Plasek, J. W. & Allard, J. (1984). Misconceptions of homophobia. *Journal of*

Homosexuality may also be viewed as a threat — either to oneself, to others, to "morality," or to society as a whole.[43] Some commentators have concluded that fear of homosexuality arises from deeply buried fears that one may have homosexual desires or fantasies. Brutal beatings or murders of gay men and lesbians, in fact — the most violent expression of homophobia — may be psychologically motivated to stamp out the attacker's own homosexual feelings.

Not infrequently, the most vehemently anti-homosexual individuals admit that they are not acquainted with anyone who is lesbian or gay.[44] But a crucial distinction should be made here. Virtually everyone *knows* homosexuals — although he or she may not be aware of the fact. Lesbians and gay men occupy every walk of life and are part of nearly every family. The mail carrier, grocery store clerk, police officer, bus driver, football star, secretary, mechanic, or minister — any of them may be homosexual. Similarly, one's uncle, wife, grandmother, child, or brother-in-law may also be gay or lesbian.

At the same time, however, many (perhaps most) homosexuals are careful not to reveal their sexual identity to others, especially their own relatives. One result is that homosexuals remain a largely invisible minority, despite the persistent belief that lesbians and gay men are easily identified by their appearance and behavior.

Hidden lesbians and gay men are, however, quite literally everywhere. When movie star Rock Hudson revealed in 1985 that he was stricken with AIDS, for example, many Americans were as shocked to realize that Hudson was gay as they were to learn that he was ill.

Homosexuality, 10(1/2), 23-37, pp. 26-27.

[44]   Millham, J., San Miguel, C. L., & Kellogg, R. (1976). A factor-analytic conceptualization of attitudes toward male and female homosexuals. *Journal of Homosexuality*, 2(1), 3-10.

There can be no doubt, of course, that the invisibility of so many lesbians and gay men contributes to widespread stereotypes and fears. Stereo-types persist precisely because heterosexuals seldom notice homosexuals who *don't* reflect their preconceptions. On the other hand, the animosity that many otherwise well-intentioned people hold toward homosexuals is ample justification for many lesbians and gay men to remain "in the closet."

Anti-homosexual sentiments, of course, act as a social control mechanism, and one of their purposes is to discourage gay people from becoming more visible. A related speculation is that the major social function of homophobia is to preserve and promote power hierarchies that are based on traditional sex-roles. As one sociologist noted,

> Homophobia is a threat used...to enforce social conformity in the male role, and maintain social control. The taunt, "What are you, a fag?" is used in many ways to encourage certain types of male behavior and to define the limits of "acceptable" masculinity.[45]

In his examination of attitudes toward gay men and lesbians, Dennis Altman identified three discrete levels of anti-homosexual prejudice — persecution, discrimination, and tolerance. Regarding the last of these three, Altman remarked:

> The real mark of tolerance is its failure to imagine the experience of others. I am constantly made aware that even the most liberal of straights thinks of a world that is entirely heterosexual, rather as there are few whites who really comprehend that for millions of Americans this is not a white country.... Tolerance, too, tends to result from an ideological position which over-rides an emotional

---

[45] Lehne, G. K. (1976). Homophobia among men. In D. S. David & R. Brannon (Eds.), *The forty-nine percent majority: The male sex role* (pp. 66-88). Reading, MA: Addison-Wesley Pub. Co., p. 78.

attitude; that is, most intelligent heterosexuals reject, intellectually, their hostility to homosexuals while [they remain] unable to conquer their emotional repugnance. The outward result is tolerance.[46]

Tolerance, as Altman describes it, is one aspect of what some commentators have called "heterosexism" or "the heterosexual bias," but there are other manifestations as well. One of the greatest difficulties non-gay people have in exploring their attitudes toward lesbians and gay men, for example, lies in being unable to look beyond the label "homosexual." Few heterosexuals realize the myriad ways in which they categorize and "pigeonhole" homosexuals on the basis of the images that are conjured up, intentionally or not, by the terms "lesbian" and "gay." It is, of course, human nature to make generalizations, and generalizations are not always harmful. When a stereotype of a group of people becomes the lens through which each and every member of the group is viewed, however — and when the lens will not or cannot be put down — then generalizations do interfere with human relations.

San Francisco Municipal Court Judge Mary Morgan, the first open lesbian appointed to the bench in the United States, put it this way: "I want people to know I'm a lesbian, but I can't stand it when the only thing they know about me is that I'm a lesbian."[47]

One effect of heterosexual bias, of course, is to distort the ways in which information about lesbians and gay men is perceived, processed, and recalled. For example, a person may read newspaper accounts of scores of crimes, but remember the details of only those committed by homosexuals. Or one may, in the course of a Sunday stroll in the park, encounter dozens of heterosexual couples walking arm-in-arm, hugging, or even necking in the grass, but what suddenly seizes the attention is a pair of women holding hands.

---

[46] Altman, D. (1973). *Homosexual oppression and liberation.* NY: Discus Books (Avon). (Original work published 1971), p.54.

[47] JEB (Joan E. Biren). (1987). *Making a way: Lesbians out front.* Washington, D.C.: Glad Hag Books (Aunt Lute), n.p.

Heterosexual bias is often evident in the media, too. Each year, for example, lesbians and gay men in many American cities commemorate the anniversary of the Stonewall uprising with parades and public celebrations. By far, the largest of these gatherings takes place in San Francisco, where parade contingents include gay accountants; lesbian doctors; gay fathers; lesbian and gay speakers of Esperanto; gay nurses; gay and lesbian students; alliances of gay and lesbian Asians, Blacks, Hispanics, Pacific Islanders, and other ethnic groups; lesbian and gay elected officials, including judges and city supervisors; the heterosexual parents and children of lesbians and gay men; and many, many others.

Media coverage, however, invariably neglects these "mainstream" individuals, who actually make up the bulk of the parade. Instead, newspaper and television accounts emphasize what reporters apparently consider the "freakish" aspects of the parade, focusing disproportionately on men in "glittering dresses" and "female bikers with cigarettes dangling from their lips."[48]

Shocked reactions from heterosexual bystanders are also popular reportage, as in this example: "I'm amazed (said a New York tourist). There was this one guy wearing handcuffs, chains, and leather. I guess he was into S&M or something."[49]

The hidden biases behind such accounts may be more easily revealed if the tables are turned a bit. Suppose, for example, that we visited a "typical" heterosexual gathering — say, a baseball game. There we might observe heterosexual couples in ill-fitting outfits of pastel polyester; voluptuous young women in halter tops and too-tight shorts; male-female pairs kissing passionately in the bleachers; heterosexual men pinching their wives' bottoms; and drunken straight men and women shouting obscenities to players on the field.

---

[48] Swan, G. A. (1982, June 28). Big SF gay parade. *San Francisco Chronicle*, A-1, A-18, p. A-1.

[49] *Ibid.*, p. A-18.

No one, however, not even a reporter, would think of describing a crowd of baseball fans in such a way. No one would focus on their "outlandish" behavior or "provocative" clothing, and no one would criticize the "flagrant" displays of sexuality. Yet, when mainstream media report on public lesbian and gay events, they frequently make precisely these sorts of "colorful" observations. The full range of lesbian and gay humanity that is always present at such gatherings — including women, men, children, people of color, stockbrokers, lawyers, pipefitters, people in wheelchairs, grandparents, and cab drivers — is virtually never acknowledged.

These are examples of the heterosexual bias at work. One's *way of seeing*, that is, significantly affects what is seen.

Imagining the Shoe on the Other Foot: A Jaundiced View of the Heterosexual "Lifestyle"

What would life be like if the only available view of *heterosexuals* was one distorted by the biases of *homosexual* society and its media? What images of *heterosexuality* would be offered in magazines and newspapers, on television shows and in movies? Consider these actual news stories — edited to promote an anti-heterosexual agenda.

> In early 1989, a jealous heterosexual winery worker in Northern California went on a rampage, *murdering his wife and two of his own children,* as well as a male co-worker whom he accused of having had an affair with his wife.

> During 1987, *American security was seriously compromised* as heterosexual Marine guards at the U.S. Embassy in Moscow involved themselves in sexual liaisons with Soviet female prostitutes — most of whom had been sent to the Embassy specifically to engage in espionage.

> Between 1980 and 1981 a male-and-female *team of heterosexuals kidnapped, sexually molested, and murdered* at least eight young women across three western states in order to fulfill the man's bizarre heterosexual fantasies. The woman helped her

straight lover by acting as a decoy to lure victims to him.

Sociological and psychological studies, too, could be distorted to put the worse possible face on heterosexual relations:

> A 1981 UCLA study of heterosexual high school students in the Los Angeles area revealed that 54 percent of boys and 42 percent of girls believed it was acceptable, in certain instances, for a man to *force a woman to have sex with him.*[50]

> A study of members of a heterosexual "swinger's club" showed that a significant proportion were "seriously emotionally disturbed, may be substance abusers, or may have *serious sexual problems.*"[51]

> In a study of the sexual behavior of 106,000 women, a respected researcher noted that 54 percent of married heterosexual women reported one or more *sexual experiences with partners other than their husbands* since marrying.[52] In another study of 7,239 men, *nearly three-fourths* of the heterosexual men who had been married two years or more had been *unfaithful while married.*[53]

> According to one study, *26 percent of all heterosexual women have been raped* — 46 percent of the victims were assaulted by friends and *seven percent by their own husbands!*[54]

---

[50] Moss, Denise. (1981, March 19). Women abused in horror films. *Phoenix* (San Francisco State University), 14.

[51] Duckworth, J. & Levitt, E. B. (1985). Personality analysis of a swinger's club. *Lifestyles, 8*(1), 34-45.

[52] Wolf, L. (1981). *The Cosmo report.* NY: Arbor House.

[53] Hite, S. (1981). *The Hite report on male sexuality.* NY: Alfred A. Knopf.

[54] Wolf, *supra.*

> A recent report concluded that *college fraternities may be a training ground for rapists!* Fraternities' emphases on "militant heterosexuality," heavy drinking, violence, hyper-masculinity, and dominance over women *actually encourage members to force women to have sex with them.* A direct consequence, the study concluded, is the dramatic increase in acquaintance rape on American campuses.[55]

Finally, imagine what might happen if information such as the above were misused by a group attempting to advance an *anti-heterosexual* political agenda. One result might be the kind of inflammatory fundraising letter that is today a favorite tool of the anti-homosexual right:

> Dear Friend:
>
> You have seen ample evidence of the violence, emotional instability, and perversion that typify the lives of heterosexuals. The rapid spread of sexually transmitted diseases among heterosexuals (including herpes, for which there is no known cure!), as well as the staggering number of elective abortions performed annually in the U.S. demonstrate that heterosexuals are not capable of conducting their sexual affairs with even a modicum of responsibility.
>
> We know, furthermore, that the crimes of rape, incest, child molestation, and spouse battering are on the rise — and that they are committed by heterosexuals in numbers vastly disproportionate to their presence in the population!
>
> In addition, the astonishing incidence of sexual harassment and sex discrimination in the work place is compelling evidence that the presence of

---

[55]   Martin, P. Y. & Hummer, R. A. (1989). Fraternities and rape on campus. *Gender and Society, 3(4),* 457-473.

heterosexuals on the job contributes to poor morale, and has a severely negative impact on job performance....[56]

And so it might go. Clearly, these tongue-in-cheek examples wouldn't convince anyone that heterosexual men and women were promiscuous, violent, morally reprehensible individuals — even though the incidents described and the statistics cited are all true. We personally know so many exceptions to these portrayals that the negative characterizations fail to be meaningful. If, on the other hand, "homosexual" were substituted for "heterosexual" in the examples above, a great many people would be prepared to accept just these sorts of gross generalizations. That, too, is the heterosexual bias at work.

Lisa Steinberg and Nathan Moncrieff

One relevant illustration of the effects of homophobia can be found in official responses to the deaths of Lisa Steinberg and Nathan Moncrieff, two children tragically murdered, within a year and a half of one another, at opposite ends of the country. Most people recall news accounts of the beating death of six-year-old Lisa Steinberg in New York City in November 1987, and the subsequent trial of her "adoptive" parents, Joel Steinberg and Hedda Nussbaum.

In fact, Steinberg and Nussbaum were not married and Lisa was never formally adopted by either of them. Instead, Lisa was placed privately with Nussbaum and Steinberg by the birth mother's obstetrician. The obstetrician and Steinberg, himself a lawyer, apparently falsified hospital documents and intimidated the birth mother into releasing Lisa to them without signing a

---

[56]   This fabricated letter is modeled on fundraising appeals and "emergency advisories" sent regularly by Jerry Falwell, the Religious Roundtable, some members of the U. S. Congress, and others with similar agendas. *See* Conway, F. & Siegleman, J. (1982). *Holy terror: The fundamentalist war on America's freedoms in religion, politics, and our private lives.* New York: Doubleday and Company.

consent or any other adoption papers. By failing to report Lisa's presence in their home or their intention to adopt her, Nussbaum and Steinberg actually violated no law.[57]

One legal analyst explained:

> In a private placement, it is not uncommon for natural parents to turn over physical custody of the adoptive child to the proposed adoptive parents at the time that an extra-judicial consent to adoption is executed. At this stage, an adoption proceeding will not have been commenced and the court will not be aware of the adoption, let alone have made any inquiry into the fitness of the prospective parents.[58]

As a result, Lisa Steinberg "fell through the cracks" of New York's independent adoption law, a fact that came to light only after her death.

Some 17 months before Lisa died, an infant named Nathan Moncrieff was beaten to death in Oakland, California by his foster parents, who were in the process of adopting him. It was quickly revealed that his foster parents were not a married couple as the DSS had believed. Instead, both parties were men — one of them a transvestite posing as the other man's wife.

New York and Oakland Respond

Following Lisa Steinberg's murder, New York quickly took steps to "seal the crack" in its adoption system. As Silverman reports, New York amended its Domestic Relations Law

> to assure that all private placement adoptions are brought quickly into court after custody has been transferred so that the court may assess the propri-

---

[57]   Silverman, C. S. (1989). Regulating independent adoptions. *Columbia Journal of Law and Social Problems, 22*(3), 323-355.

[58]   *Ibid.*, p. 338.

ety of the temporary guardianship by the prospective adoptive parents.[59]

In specific, the amended law gives the prospective adoptive parents, as temporary guardians of a child placed with them privately, 10 days to file a petition either for guardianship or for adoption. The court, in addition, is required to act promptly to assess the home and to decide whether to grant the temporary guardianship.[60] As Silverman notes, however, the amendment "will not improve the ability of officials to detect potential adoptive parents who willfully fail to file this petition."[61]

Other recommendations have been made, but not yet approved, to eliminate "baby brokering" in all its forms, to make extra-judicial consents to adoption by birth mothers illegal, to limit the ability of unauthorized individuals to "place" a child informally for adoption, and other strategies.[62]

In Oakland, California, in contrast, in the wake of Nathan Moncrieff's death, probes of the foster care and Fost-Adopt programs were initiated in Alameda County (of which Oakland is a part), and neighboring San Francisco County. A series of reports in the *San Francisco Chronicle* revealed other incidents of abuse and neglect in foster homes and criticized the Department's "minimal" procedures for the screening of foster parents.[63]

Within a matter of months, the California Department of Social Services had developed a new adoption policy, based in part on the Moncrieff tragedy. The policy stated:

> The best interests of [adoptive children] are served by placement in homes where the couple demonstrates a deep commitment to permanency.

---

[59]   *Ibid.*

[60]   *Ibid.*

[61]   *Ibid.*, p. 339.

[62]   *Ibid.*, pp. 339-340.

[63]   Wallace, B. & Stone, A. (1986, July 22). Trouble with foster homes. *San Francisco Chronicle*, 1, 4-5.

Couples who have formalized their relationship
through a legal marriage reflect this desired commitment.

One of the first cases to be affected by the new policy involved
a lesbian mother who wished to co-adopt her partner's child, a 4-
year-old girl whom they had both co-parented since the child's
birth.[64] It is true, in fact, that at least two lesbian-couple joint
adoptions had been approved earlier in 1986, one in Alameda and
one in San Francisco County.[65] This third adoption, however, was
still making its way through the San Francisco DSS when Moncrieff was killed, at a time when the Department had apparently
become quite sensitive to possible criticism for its approval of gay
and lesbian adoptions. Since lesbians and gay men cannot legally
marry their partners, of course, some felt that the marital-status
policy was nothing more than an attempt to screen out such
couples.

Whatever the DSS's intentions, ironically, the new policy
could not have prevented Moncrieff's death — even if it had been
in place prior to June of 1986. Moncrieff's foster parents presented
themselves as a married couple and were approved as a married
couple. What went wrong with the Moncrieff placement was that
the Alameda County DSS failed to follow its own screening
procedures. As one Bay Area, California adoption attorney noted:

Apparently, [the DSS] didn't even run a routine
fingerprint check [on Moncrieff's foster parents],
which would have revealed the fact that the parents were both men and that one of them had a
criminal record.

Indeed, rather than focus on the ways in which Nathan Moncrieff "fell through the cracks" of the California adoption system,
and thus on the system's inadequacies, the DSS chose to concen-

---

[64]   *In the Matter of the Adoption Petition of N.* (California Superior Court, San
Francisco County, March 11, 1986), No. 18086.

[65]   No. 17945 (California Superior Court, San Francisco County, February 24,
1986); No. 17350 (California Superior Court, Alameda County, April 8, 1986).

trate on the homosexual issue — in specific, on the fact that a legal marriage could not have taken place between the two men.

The result was a double disaster for children: Not only were some children to be denied the advantages of having two legal parents (when their parents were both men or both women),[66] but all children suffered from the DSS's failure to address its weaknesses directly and to remedy them.

It is interesting to speculate how New York might have responded if Lisa Steinberg had been abused and killed by gay or lesbian parents. It is, in any case, likely that Joel Steinberg's and Hedda Nussbaum's heterosexuality was the factor that allowed New York to address the genuine failings in its system, rather than to be misled by sensationalized issues. Although its response remains imperfect, New York may, in the end, prove to have fashioned the more competent response to tragedy.

Homophobia in the Wider View

Any discussion of the role of lesbians and gay men in foster parenting programs must include a consideration of the negative attitudes many people continue to hold toward them. There is, of course, no means by which individuals can be made to set aside their anti-homosexual beliefs or to consider the possibility that society might benefit from a re-examination of its treatment of gay men and lesbians.

Furthermore, we have no national strategy for counteracting homophobia that is similar to our policies against racial prejudice, gender-based discrimination, and other forms of social disenfranchisement. In many cases, in fact, the law neither protects homosexuals nor requires that their dignity or their rights be safeguarded by others.

---

[66] In the years since, attorneys have successfully challenged the marital-status policy on several occasions and have obtained decrees of adoption for gay or lesbian couples, despite the official objections of the California DSS. Millie Jessen and Sue Pavlik's joint adoption of Eric was one such case.

We can, however, require of ourselves and our colleagues an intellectual rigor that prevents assumptions from being deemed as worthy as facts, and inherited prejudices from being considered as valuable as direct experience.

Although gay men and lesbians experience considerable prejudice today, their social and legal situation will not always remain as now. America has, in its history, made a remarkable commitment to fulfilling one of its most honorable promises — "justice for all." Along the way, America's policy-makers have sometimes had to reassess their attitudes and jettison their former positions. Occasionally, too, our laws and social policies have been slow to condemn bias and to remedy its effect.

Experience teaches us, nonetheless, that the progress of history has never vindicated the prejudices of earlier times. In considering the many difficult questions raised by lesbian and gay foster parenting, that awareness may be one of our most valuable tools.

CHAPTER THREE

Prejudice Against Gay Men and Lesbians — The Influence of Religion

Prejudice against lesbians and gay men is so widespread in America, and so much a part of the social fabric, that many people see no reason to question their beliefs or to change their attitudes. This is particularly likely to be true when anti-homosexual sentiment is undergirded by conservative religious beliefs. Today, the most entrenched religious beliefs against homosexuality are held by fundamentalist Protestant groups, Eastern Orthodox churches, Orthodox Judaism, and the Roman Catholic Church.

In 1986, for example, the Vatican issued a Pastoral Letter regarding homosexuality and took this position on the subject of violent attacks against lesbians and gay men:

> [T]he proper reaction to crimes committed against homosexual persons should not be to claim that the homosexual condition is not disordered. When such a claim is made and when homosexual activity is consequently condoned, or when civil legislation is introduced to protect behavior to which no one has any conceivable right, neither the Church nor society should be surprised when other distorted notions and practices gain ground, and irrational and violent reactions increase.[67]

Although most historians believe that Christianity persecuted homosexual behavior from the earliest days of the Church, a more

---

[67] Congregation for the Doctrine of the Faith. (1986). *On the pastoral care of homosexual persons.* Boston, MA: Daughters of St. Paul, p. 8.

recent study, *Christianity, Social Tolerance and Homosexuality*,[68] argues that, for many centuries, Catholic Europe showed no particular hostility toward homosexuality. The primary impetus for the Church's modern-day position came from the writings of St. Augustine and Thomas Aquinas, who believed that all sexual acts that did not result in procreation were unnatural and sinful.

Contemporary sex educators have expanded on the notion of "reproductive bias," noting that such a bias has created a large category of individuals whose sexual and romantic needs or behavior may be defined by others as inappropriate, unnatural, unhealthy, sick, wasteful, sinful, or immoral. They call these groups the "sexually oppressed" and note that the reproductive bias lies behind many modern prohibitions — both secular and ecclesiastical — against such practices as masturbation, pre-marital sex, sex among the elderly, adolescent sexuality, and, of course, homosexuality.[69]

Of the chief American anti-homosexual campaigns in recent history, moreover, all have taken religious precepts as a major justification for their convictions. Anita Bryant's 1977 "Save Our Children" crusade is one example. More recently, when an ordinance recognizing lesbian-and-gay family partnerships was approved in San Francisco in 1989, organized opposition to the ordinance was inaugurated, during Mother's Day Sunday services, by a petition drive in several local evangelical churches.[70]

Several passages in the Bible or the Torah are generally cited as condemnation of homosexual behavior. A few essential points should be made here with regard to scriptural and religious justifications for anti-homosexual attitudes or laws.

---

[68] Boswell, J. (1980). *Christianity, social tolerance, and homosexuality.* Chicago: University of Chicago Press.

[69] On the problems of the sexually oppressed generally, and social work efforts to relieve those problems, *See* Gochros, H. L. & Gochros, J. S. (1977). *The sexually oppressed.* NY: Association Press; and Gochros, H. L., Gochros, J. S., & Fischer, J. L. (1986). *Helping the sexually oppressed.* Englewood Cliffs, NJ: Prentice-Hall.

[70] Israels, D. (1989, October 18). Domestic partners: Too close to call. *San Francisco Bay Guardian, 23,* 30.

1.   *Despite the claims of some religious fundamentalists, significa.* *questions remain today regarding the meaning and historical context of* *many scriptural passages.* Most people are aware that the Bible has been translated and revised constantly over the last two thousand years. In an exhaustive article regarding issues facing contemporary Bible scholars, Hoberman noted that the English-language Bible has been modified and re-translated literally scores of times since the popular King James Version appeared in the early 1600s.[71] In tracing the many and varied problems of translation and interpretation facing Bible scholars and translators, Hoberman writes,

> We have no original text of any biblical book, and some books may have circulated in more than one version almost from the beginning of their existence as written documents.... To further complicate matters, all the books of the Bible have to some degree suffered the textual corruption that is the inevitable by-product of two to three thousand years of manuscript copying and recopying.[72]

Hoberman goes on to explain that:

> Virtually everything having to do with the Bible is more complicated, more ambiguous and open to debate, than most Christians and Jews — even educated church and synagogue members — are aware of. To put it another way, too many people give too many easy answers to questions about the Bible. This is true not only with respect to...Bible translation, but also with respect to the history of biblical times and the theology of the Scriptures.[73]

As Hoberman also points out, translations and re-editions of the Bible commonly evince the theological and even political

---

[71]   Hoberman, B. (1985, February). Translating the Bible: An endless task. *Atlantic Monthly*, 43-51, 54-58.

[72]   *Ibid.*, p. 47.

[73]   *Ibid.*, p. 58.

...ases of the preparators. This is perhaps nowhere more true, ...an with respect to the Living Bible, which Hoberman reports "really does not deserve to be called a translation." He adds,

> [M]any evangelical and fundamentalist Christians ... have made [the Living Bible] their Bible of choice, holding it to be a valid alternative to other versions of the Scriptures. However, in numerous places, the Living Bible actually distorts the biblical message.[74]

But what have these considerations about translation, historical accuracy, and interpretation to do with the issue of homosexuality? First, it is essential to recognize that a significant body of biblical scholars now agrees on two important points: (1) that scriptural injunctions against homosexuality may refer to historical and cultural phenomena that were nothing like the lives of modern-day gay men and lesbians and (2) that the very words that have been assumed to refer to homosexuality may, in fact, have been mistranslated. (Bailey[75] and McNeill,[76] for example, have written extensively on scholarly reinterpretations of the famous Sodom and Gomorrah story, among other things.)

At the very least, questions regarding translation of the Scriptures and ambiguities in reconstructing their original historical context and meaning are leading some religious leaders to soften their attitudes toward homosexuality. Dialogue on the subject has opened within many churches today, and some are rejecting strict anti-homosexual interpretations of scripture. There is, moreover, acceptance within some denominations of the ordination of lesbian and gay clergy, and the debate over this issue will certainly continue.

---

[74]   *Ibid.*, p. 55.

[75]   Bailey, D. S. (1975). *Homosexuality and the Western Christian tradition.* Hamden, CT: Archon Books. (Original work published 1955)

[76]   McNeill, J. J. (1976). *The Church and the homosexual.* Kansas City, MO: Sheed Andrews and McMeel, Inc.

2. *Inasmuch as scripture has historically been used to justify and condone various forms of oppression, we should be cautious of exclusively religious rationales for anti-homosexual prejudice.* Religion has served political aims on more than one occasion in America's history. Many Americans don't realize, for example, that deep theological and political schisms were occasioned in American churches by the slavery debate prior to and during the Civil War.

Slavery was widely defended on the ground that, because "the New Testament nowhere condemns slaveholding...then to pronounce slaveholding to be in itself sinful is contrary to Scriptures."[77] Indeed, the Bible contains many passages that can be (and were) interpreted as condoning the institution of slavery, including Leviticus 25: 44-46, which reads:

> Slaves, male and female, you may indeed possess, provided you buy them from among the neighboring nations. You may also buy them from among the aliens who reside with you.... Such slaves you may own as chattels, and leave to your sons as their hereditary property....

Related passages include Ephesians 6:5-8 ("Slaves, obey your masters according to the flesh, with fear and trembling in the sincerity of your heart, as you would Christ"), Titus 2:9-10 ("Exhort slaves to obey their masters, pleasing them in all things and not opposing them"), as well as I Timothy 6:1-2, and Colossians 3:22-24.

Among the pro-slavery voices raised during those years was that of South Carolina Governor Hammond. Quoting from the Bible and condemning the abolitionist movement, Hammond declared, "God created Negroes for no other purpose than to be subordinate 'hewers of wood and drawers of water' — that is, to be slaves to the white race."[78] Hammond's appeal to godliness as a justification for racism is echoed today in the biblical precedent

---

[77] Edel, W. (1987). *Defenders of the faith: Religion and politics from the pilgrim fathers to Ronald Reagan.* NY: Praeger Press, p. 90.

[78] *Ibid.*

claimed by Jerry Falwell, Jesse Helms, William Dannemeyer, and others for their anti-homosexual stance.[79]

Women, too, have fared poorly in debates that depend upon literalist interpretations of the Scriptures. Women are described in I Peter 3:7, for example, as "the weaker vessel." Elsewhere, women are advised to "learn in silence with all submission. For I do not allow a women to teach or to exercise authority over men; but she is to keep quiet. For Adam was formed first, then Eve" (I Timothy 11-14). Women are exhorted to "keep silence in the churches, for it is not permitted them to speak.... But if they want to learn anything, let them ask their husbands at home...." (I Corinthians 14:34-35). Finally, in Paul's letter to the Colossians, his instruction to wives is "[B]e subject to your husbands, as is becoming in the Lord" (Colossians 3:18). The common apologia that these views toward women are "old-fashioned" — and therefore less compelling today —should logically apply to scriptural injunctions against homosexuality as well.

There are, of course, numerous problems inherent in "text-proofing" — that is, the practice of pulling out Bible verses to support particular points of view. Although Christian fundamentalists are particularly inclined to argue in favor of a literal and "infallible" Bible, and are quick to cite scriptural "proofs" for their positions, a more reasoned approach recognizes that many questions about the scriptures (and, indeed, about modern morality) remain unanswered.

Scholar Daniel Maguire, for example, notes that the literalist position

> would make it difficult to explain that verse in Deuteronomy that says that a virgin who is raped must marry her attacker (22:28-29).... In the Bible's

---

[79] Biblical justification for racism is not limited to the civil war period or to the antebellum slavery debate, however. In Idaho today, the Reverend Richard Butler trains neo-Nazi skinheads at his 20-acre compound near Hayden Lake. Playing the part of "the kindly preacher," Butler "shrouds his racist message in religion, using scripture to support his claims of white supremacy." *See* Foster, D. (1989, April 23). Aryan preacher woos skinheads. *San Francisco Examiner*, A-3.

view [he continues] if you have a stubborn and rebellious son...the parents should denounce him publicly and 'then all this fellow citizens shall stone him to death' (Deuteronomy 21:18-21).[80]

Among the other biblical laws ignored by anti-homosexual religious are prohibitions against all contact with a menstruating woman (Leviticus 15:19-24); against charging interest on a loan (Deuteronomy 23:20); against a man's trimming his beard (Leviticus 19:27); and against soothsaying, divination, and consulting fortunetellers (Leviticus 19:27, 31) — a rule that even Nancy Reagan apparently overlooked. The Bible also instructs men regarding the manner in which they may marry or divorce a slave (Deuteronomy 21:10-14).

Notably, all of these laws are found near the same sections of the Old Testament where appear the passages generally cited in condemnation of homosexuality (Genesis 19:1-22, Leviticus 18:22 and 20:13). It is not clear why religious conservatives ignore the bulk of the Old Testament's many, detailed laws regarding diet, daily and family life, cleanliness, agriculture, and finance while putting so much emphasis on so-called anti-homosexual passages. Indeed, Maguire argues, "[E]ven [the New Right] shows, by what they ignore in the Bible, that the Bible requires interpretation."[81]

More significantly, even assuming that injunctions against homosexuality, *as we know it today*, can be inferred from the Scriptures, it is important to recognize (a) that homosexuality is discussed no more than four times in the Bible, whereas other sexual sins, including adultery and lust, are mentioned repeatedly; (b) that prohibitions against non-sexual sins, such as greed, envy, and drunkenness are much more common than those against sexual sins, including homosexuality; and (c) that Jesus is not reported to have mentioned a single word about homosexuality, although He otherwise had a great deal to say about the nature and breadth of human sinfulness.

---

[80]   Maguire, D. C. (1982). *The new subversives: Anti-Americanism and the Religious Right.* NY: Continuum Publishing Company, p. 60

[81]   *Ibid.*, p. 61.

Given these considerations, it seems appropriate to ask: If homosexuality is as significant and loathsome a sin as members of the religious right insist, why is it not given greater and clearer emphasis in the Scriptures?

3. *Regardless of debates over the significance and meaning of Judeo-Christian theology and anti-homosexual traditions, religious considerations are meant to play a limited role in the framing of our country's laws.* Perhaps needless to say, all Americans do not subscribe to the same set of religious or moral values. Religious freedom; freedom of speech; separation of church and state; and the rights to life, liberty and the pursuit of happiness are four of our country's most cherished principles. They do not, however, always co-exist in perfect harmony. Our courts and our legislatures are constantly struggling to achieve compromises between individuals' self-defined concepts of right living, on the one hand, and access to America's opportunities, resources, and legal protections, on the other.

It may be neither possible nor desirable to separate "church" completely from the operations of the "state," but it cannot become the function of government to enforce one set of religious standards over all others. Although we are a nation "under God," we are also a government "of and for the people," and that is an equilibrium we must always strive to maintain.

Those who hold strong religious beliefs, of course, are not necessarily anti-homosexual. What is more, the Christian principle of love for one's fellow human beings can also soften the workings of prejudice. This issue was on the minds of some scholars even before the modern gay liberation movement began to encourage a new consideration of homosexuality and religious life. As early as 1966, one theologian wrote:

> Where is the good news which the Church claims
> to offer to all men, regardless of their sins? Where
> is the message that Christ is the redeemer of all
> men? The Church has failed at the most basic level
> and in its dealings with the homosexual, by failing
> to recognize him as a human being who is sacred in
> the sight of God. Until those within the Church can

> learn to overcome their aversion to the homosex-
> ual, there can be no dialogue, and the homosexual
> will feel shut out of the House of God.[82]

In addition, in recent years a large number of religious organizations have officially declared their support for their homosexual members and for the struggle of lesbians and gay men to obtain equal rights.. These include the Episcopal Church, the National Council of Churches of Christ, the Lutheran Church in America, the Society of Friends (Quakers), the American Jewish Congress, the Unitarian Universalist Association, the American Rabbinical Assembly, the National Federation of Priest Councils, the Union of American Hebrew Congregations, and others.[83]

Child welfare managers must, of course, be aware of the strong feelings of people who are anti-homosexual. Such individuals do not want children placed with lesbians and gay men because they fear the children will be harmed — either physically, morally, or spiritually. Their beliefs are deeply rooted in a lifetime of instruction that homosexuality is wrong and sinful. The people such individuals respect most highly — their parents, their pastors or rabbis, even their political leaders — often hold virulently anti-homosexual beliefs.

The changing of homophobic attitudes requires individuals to undergo careful reconsideration of their value and belief structures. If they are to modify their anti-homosexual biases, they will have to reject some of what they have learned, leave some of what they have been taught intact, and expand their value systems to include new experiences and possibilities.

For those interested in exploring alternative approaches to homosexuality and religion, a bibliography is provided in Appendix A.

---

[82]   Jones, H. K. (1966). *Toward a Christian understanding of the homosexual.* NY: Association Press, pp. 102-103.

[83]   Polikoff, *supra*, p. 550, fn. 510; *see also* Conservative Rabbis call for gay rights. (1990, June). *Lesbian/Gay Law Notes*, p. 41.

CHAPTER FOUR

Parenting by Lesbians and Gay Men — Typical Concerns and a Review of the Literature

Few topics conjure up the gut-level fears that are evoked when homosexuals are proposed as teachers, caretakers, or parents of children. Even individuals who are generally supportive of lesbian and gay civil rights seem to draw the line at contact with children. A recent Gallup poll, for example, found that 71 percent of respondents believed gays and lesbians "should have equal rights in terms of job opportunities." Only 42 percent, however, felt the same way when the job in question was that of elementary school teacher.[84]

In Massachusetts, as another example, Governor Michael Dukakis repeatedly refused all requests to modify or eliminate the restrictive provisions of his state's 1985 foster care policy as it related to homosexuals. In November, 1989, however, Dukakis signed a bill into law that made Massachusetts one of only two states with statewide civil rights protections for lesbians and gay men (e.g., in employment, housing, and public accommodations).

Among the common fears and stereotypes related to homosexuals and children are these: that lesbians and gay men are mentally ill, unstable, or irresponsible; that lesbians and especially gay men are sexually perverted and will engage in sexual activity in front of children; that same-sex couples assume exaggerated male and female roles; that lesbian or gay parents or their friends or partners will molest children; that the children of homosexual parents grow up to be confused in their gender identity and are likely to become homosexual themselves; that children will be

---

[84]   Kagay, M. R. (1989, October 25). Homosexuals gain more acceptance. *New York Times*, A-24.

socially stigmatized as a result of living in a lesbian or gay household; and that children are harmed by witnessing affectionate behavior between two persons of the same sex.

Indeed, since the late 1950s and through the 1970s, researchers have repeatedly demonstrated that non-clinical groups of lesbians and gay men can in no way be differentiated from their heterosexual counterparts on a variety of measures of psychological health, adjustment, and well-being.[85] The pioneering research of psychologist Evelyn Hooker in this area was so exceptional, in fact, that a documentary of Hooker's life and work — *Changing Our Minds* — was scheduled for public-television broadcast in 1990.[86]

Most helping professionals are now aware, moreover, that more than 16 years have passed since both the American Psychological Association and the American Psychiatric Association removed homosexuality from diagnostic lists of mental illness. These decisions came after extensive discussions, a massive literature review and, finally, a determination that no scientific basis existed for the continued pathologization of homosexuality. Prior to the removal of homosexuality from the *Diagnostic and Statistical Manual* in 1973, for example, the full Nomenclature Committee of the American Psychiatric Association received a report which stated, in part, "[T]here is not one objective study, by any researcher, in any country, that substantiates the theory of homosexual pathology," and concluded that research data

---

[85] *See,* e.g., Hooker, E. (1956). A preliminary analysis of group behavior of homosexuals. *Journal of Psychology, 42,* 217-25; Hooker, E. (1957). The adjustment of the male overt homosexual. *Journal of Projective Techniques, 21*(1), 18-31; Hooker, E. (1969). Parental relations and male homosexuality in patient and nonpatient samples. *Journal of Consulting and Clinical Psychology, 33*(2), 140-142; and Seligman, M. (1972). Adjustment of homosexual and heterosexual women. *British Journal of Psychiatry, 120,* 477-481. *See* also summaries in Paul, W., Weinrich, J. D., Gonsiorek, J. C. & Hotvedt, M. E. (Eds.), *Homosexuality: Social, psychological, and biological issues.* Beverly Hills, CA: Sage.

[86] Information is available from the Foundation for Integral Studies, 123 W. 44th Street, Garden Level - A, New York, NY 10036, 212/354-6840.

compelled the conclusion that "homosexuality falls within the normal range of psychological functioning."[87]

In fact, virtually every myth related to lesbian and gay parenting has likewise been refuted by modern social science; yet fears about homosexual parenting have proven remarkably resilient.[88] In analyzing such resistance, American University College of Law Professor Nancy Polikoff[89] provides this outstanding historical perspective:

> Courts and legislatures have previously seized on discriminatory ideologies disguised as scientific truth to serve as the basis for judicial and statutory activism in the area of child rearing. Courts that upheld laws prohibiting racial intermarriage, for example, relied on hypotheses now considered preposterous, including that "the offspring of these unnatural connections are generally sickly and effeminate, and inferior in physical development and strength to the full-blood of either race,"[90] and "it is stated as a well authenticated fact that if the issue of a black man and a white woman, and a

---

87   Silverstein, C. (1976). "Even psychiatry can profit from its past mistakes." *Journal of Homosexuality, 2(2),* 153-158, p. 157.

88   A number of legal scholars have reviewed the social science research and applied the relevant findings to myths and stereotypes about homosexuals and about gay and lesbian parenting. *See,* e.g., O'Toole, M. T. (1989). Gay parenting: Myths and realities. *Pace Law Review, 9,* 129-164; Polikoff, *supra;* Susoeff, S. (1985). Assessing children's best interests when a parent is gay or lesbian. *UCLA Law Review, 332(4),* 852-903; and Mohr, R. (1989). *Gays/justice: A study in ethics, society, and law.* NY: Columbia University Press.

89   The author is indebted to Professor Polikoff for permission to quote from her exceptionally insightful and meticulously researched article, "This Child Does Have Two Mothers: Redefining Parenthood to Meet the Needs of Children in Lesbian-Mother and Other Nontraditional Families," *supra.* The citations contained within the quotes are from Professor Polikoff's own research.

90   Polikoff, *supra,* pp. 545-546, citing *Scott v. Georgia* (1869) 39 Ga.Rep. 321 at 323.

white man and a black woman, intermarry, they cannot possibly have any progeny."[91] Support for passage of Virginia's Racial Integrity Act of 1924, which prohibited any white person from marrying any nonwhite person arose out of eugenics theories espoused by doctors offering professional expert opinions.

As recently as 1966, Virginia argued in support of its antimiscegenation laws that "[t]he available scientific materials are sufficient to support the validity of the [antimiscegenation] statute."[92] The State quoted from various medical, scientific, and psychological experts to assert that interracial marriage posed a threat to children's "welfare and to the welfare of society as well because highly charged emotional experiences often leave such children disturbed, frustrated and unable to believe that they can live normal, happy lives."[93]

The State also argued that not enough was known about the "biological consequences" of interracial marriages.[94]

It is now easy to recognize that the antimiscegenation laws were grounded in racist ideology, not scientific principles. Similarly, we can now see that sexist ideology disguised as science was the motivation behind Victorian laws that reinforced women's child-rearing role and restricted their access to public life. Because society is still firmly entrenched in homophobia and heterosexism,

---

[91]   *Ibid.*, p. 546, fn. 480, citing *State v. Jackson* (1883) 80 Mo. 175 at 179.

[92]   *Ibid.*, p. 546, fn. 483, citing *Loving v. Virginia*, 338 U.S. 1 (1967).

[93]   *Ibid.*, p. 546, citing Brief and Appendix of Appellee, pp. 10-11, quoting A. Gordon, *Intermarriage: Interfaith, Interracial, Interethnic.*

[94]   *Ibid.*, p. 546, fn. 485.

however, it is less easy to recognize that restrictions on lesbian and gay parenting are also ideologically based.[95]

Review of the literature

The scholarly literature on gay and lesbian parenting is no longer scarce. A bibliography, Appendix B, includes nearly 80 professional articles and books. Excellent summaries of the literature have been prepared by Cramer[96] and by Bozett,[97] but it is useful to review some of this material here.

Most of the relevant literature has focused on lesbian mothers and their children, although studies of gay fathers have been undertaken as well and are increasingly more common. Work remains to be done vis-a-vis foster and adoptive lesbian and gay families in particular, and more research is needed that follows the psychological development of children raised in gay or lesbian households over longer periods of time. In general, however, there is more than sufficient evidence to refute the common fears regarding lesbian and gay parents.

Although deeply entrenched beliefs will persist regarding the "immorality" and "sickness" of lesbians and gay men, social science research is answering the concerns typically raised by those who challenge lesbian and gay parenting. These findings may be summarized as follows:

1. *Homosexual and heterosexual parents do not differ in quality of parenting.* Levy found that lesbian mothers functioned

---

95 *Ibid.*, pp. 546-547.

96 Cramer, D. Gay parents and their children: A review of research and practical implications. *Journal of Counseling and Development*, 1986, *64*, 504-507.

97 Bozett, F. W. Gay fathers: A review of the literature. *Journal of Homosexuality*, 1989, *18*(1/2), 137-162.

well in spite of negative social pressures,[98] while Pagelow found lesbian mothers more independent than heterosexual mothers because they were more attuned to the effects of oppression.[99] Bigner and Jacobsen[100] found that heterosexual and homosexual fathers' motivations for becoming parents were similar and reported no differences between the two groups on a "Value of Children" measure. Although Bigner and Jacobsen also demonstrated no differences between gay and heterosexual fathers in intimacy or involvement with their children, they did note that gay fathers went to greater lengths to explain rules and regulations to their children, encouraged greater emotional expressiveness, and were more consistent than heterosexual fathers in setting and enforcing limits on children's behavior.[101]

2. *Children raised in lesbian and gay households do not differ from children raised in heterosexual households in overall mental health, adjustment, or gender identity.* Green, Mandel, Hotvedt, Gray and Smith compared a group of three-to-eleven-year-old children of lesbian mothers with a similar group of children of single heterosexual mothers. They reported,

> [I]t is clear that boys and girls raised from early
> childhood by a homosexual mother without an
> adult male in the household for about 4 years do
> not appear appreciably different on parameters of
> psychosexual and psychosocial development from

---

[98]   Levy, E. F. (1983). *Lesbian mothers' coping characteristics: An exploration of social, psychological, and family coping resources.* Unpublished doctoral dissertation, University of Wisconsin, Madison.

[99]   Pagelow, M. D. (1980). Heterosexual and lesbian single mothers: A comparison of problems, coping, and solutions. *Journal of Homosexuality, 5*(3), 180-204.

[100]   Bigner, J. J. & Jacobsen, R. B. (1989a). The value of children to gay and heterosexual fathers. *Journal of Homosexuality, 18*(1/2), 163-172; Bigner, J. J. & Jacobsen, R. B. (1989b). Parenting behaviors of homosexual and heterosexual fathers. *Journal of Homosexuality, 18*(1/2), 173-186.

[101]   Bigner & Jacobsen, 1989b, *supra.*

children raised by heterosexual mothers, also without an adult male present.[102]

In a comparison of children of divorced heterosexual and divorced lesbian mothers, Huggins reported no statistically significant differences in the self-esteem scores of the two groups of male and female children of similar ages.[103] Lewis interviewed 21 children of lesbians, ages 9 to 26. She found that the children experienced some problems and conflicts because of society's views of homosexuality and of their family constellations, but all expressed pride in the mother's bravery in declaring her sexual preference.[104] Lewin found that the lesbian mother's sexual orientation had less influence on children's well-being than other factors such as the mother's ethnicity, religion, occupation, social class, political ideology, and status as a mother.[105]

Polikoff, in her review of the relevant literature, provided this summary:

> [One] study…compared twenty-seven lesbian-mother families and twenty-seven single heterosexual-mother families. The lesbian-mother group contained thirty-seven children aged five to seventeen, and the single heterosexual-mother group contained thirty-eight children of this same age group. In evaluating psychosexual development, the researchers interviewed both mothers and children. They found no evidence of inappropriate gender identity for any of the children, and no

---

[102] Green, R., Mandel, J.B., Hotvedt, M.E., Gray, J. & Smith, L. (1986). Lesbian mothers and their children: A comparison with solo parent heterosexual mothers and their children. *Archives of Sexual Behavior, 15*(2), 167-184, p. 182.

[103] Huggins, S. L. (1989). A comparative study of self-esteem of adolescent children of divorced lesbian mothers and divorced heterosexual mothers. *Journal of Homosexuality, 18*(1/2), 123-135.

[104] Lewis, K. G. (1980). Children of lesbian parents: Their point of view. *Social Work, 25*(3), 198-203.

[105] Lewin, E. (1981). Lesbianism and motherhood: Implications for child custody. *Human Organizations, 40*, 6-14.

differences between the two groups regarding sex role behavior or sexual orientation.

The researchers also obtained information about the children's emotions, behavior, and relationships from parent and teacher questionnaires and from interviews with the mothers. This information revealed no differences between the two groups regarding the children's ability to make and maintain peer relationships and found a substantially greater number of children with significant psychiatric problems in the single heterosexual-mother group than in the lesbian-mother group.[106]

Other researchers compared 20 five-to-twelve-year-old children living in lesbian-mother families with 20 similar children raised in single heterosexual-mother families. A group of professionals (who did not know beforehand which children belonged to which family setting) evaluated the children on various playroom and psychological tests. The study found no differences between the two groups of children in psychological health or gender development.[107]

3. *Lesbian and gay parents are acutely concerned that their children may suffer because their family is different and go to considerable lengths to accommodate and respond to children's needs.* Golombok, et al. noted that lesbian mothers in their study did more than divorced or unmarried heterosexual mothers to insure that their children maintained ongoing contact with their natural fathers. Further, in contrast to stereotypes, lesbian mothers made sure

---

[106] Polikoff, *supra*, pp. 562-563, citing Golombok, S., Spencer, A. & Rutter, M. (1983). Children in lesbian and single-parent households: Psychosexual and psychiatric appraisal. *Journal of Child Psychology and Psychiatry, 24*(4), 551-572.

[107] Kirkpatrick, M., Smith, K. & Roy, D. (1981). Lesbian mothers and their children: A comparative survey. *American Journal of Orthopsychiatry, 51*, 545-551.

their children had the opportunity to form relationships with a variety of male, female, heterosexual, and homosexual adults.[108]

Therapist Saralie Pennington, who has worked extensively with lesbian-mother families, noted:

> From my observations lesbian mothers will do anything to help their children deal with their differences in a homophobic world except "go back into the closet." For example, they will be extremely careful not to show affection to a partner in front of anyone except immediate family and friends. They will be careful not to exhibit any literature, art, or home decoration that could be interpreted as lesbian-oriented. They may even encourage their children to refer to their lover as "aunt" in order to make it more comfortable for them to bring friends home. These measures often work to assuage the child's concerns and may be indicative of the mother's sensitivity and flexibility.
>
> Children's reactions to mother "coming out" generally range from "please, can't you change, you're ruining my life!" to "I'm proud of my mom, and if other kids don't like it, then I don't want that kind of person to be my friend."... The burden that the mother's lesbian orientation poses for both mother and child has positive ramifications as well, including [an] opportunity for the child to have female role models that can be strong, independent, and nurturing .... Children in these households develop an appreciation of differences and of different ways of living. They learn not to worry so much about what other people will think, and they have the potential for being more self-reliant and self-confident.[109]

---

[109]   Pennington, S. B. (1987). Children of lesbian mothers. In F. W. Bozett (Ed.), *Gay and lesbian parents* (pp. 58-74). New York: Praeger Press, pp. 65-66.

[108]   Golombok, et al., *supra*.

These same points are reinforced by the anecdotal comments of two heterosexual teenagers — a boy, 18, and a girl, 19 — raised in lesbian-parent homes. These excerpts are taken from interviews published by Ricketts and Achtenberg.[110]

Alicia

I think [lesbian and gay parents] have to be aware of their kids' need to have a "normal" house when their friends come over. For me, that was vital. To know that there are times when kids are going to want their parents not to act like they're lovers....

And they need to be really understanding about helping their kids figure out what they want to tell their friends .... I remember talking to my mom about feeling uncomfortable telling so-and-so, and having her say, "Well, just take your time. They don't have to know. Let them know when you want to tell them. There's no rush." ... If my mom had pushed me to tell people, I think I would have had a much harder time.

If my mom hadn't been a lesbian, you could say that I'd have led a more normal life. You could say that if my [original] parents hadn't gotten divorced, I'd have had a more normal life, but it would have been hell. I'm actually glad because I don't think I'm nearly as naive as I would have been .... I can get along with anybody, and I don't make judgments unless someone hurts me or does something I don't like. I get along with a lot more diverse crowd than most of my friends.

Basically, I have two of the greatest parents, and I find it hard when people judge them by what their sexual preference is. What I see from me and [other friends with gay parents] is that we're a lot more comfortable around adults, that we appear a lot more grown up in terms of responsibility and leadership. I'm much more supportive of women, too, and now that I can vote, I'm

---

[110]   Ricketts & Achtenberg, 1990, *supra*, pp. 90-93.

more aware of what I want to vote for. And it may very well have something to do with having grown up in this family.

Dave

I think what's important is if parents just explain, [as my lesbian parents did], that they weren't trying to pressure me to be gay at all, that it was strictly my decision and they weren't even going to have anything to do with it. They always encouraged me to go out with girls and stuff. And my mom taught me how to be independent, which was really important to me. I don't know whether that has anything to do with having gay parents, but it's one thing parents should teach anyway.

I think parents should respect what their kids are going through, too. Because in a sense they do put their son or daughter in an awkward position. I mean, it's not like a life-or-death situation, but it does put pressure on a kid, and it's something that they obviously have to live with. And I'd tell them pretty early, so they know why their family's different.

I guess it was more on my mind when I was younger that I might turn out to be gay, too. I never told anybody about my parents then, because I felt if they knew, they would stereotype me as being gay because of them. I think I used to make it more of a problem in my head than it ever actually was. Now I feel like if my friends can't deal with it, then that's their problem, because I'm not worried about my reputation anymore.

It seems to me that basically I have a family here, and it doesn't seem much different from any other person's family, except that some people don't accept it as a family. The only problem I ever had was just having to deal with other people dealing with my lifestyle.

Child Molestation

Anita Bryant's 1977 campaign against a Dade County, Florida gay rights ordinance — a crusade many will recall by the name "Save Our Children" — was one of the most remarkable attempts in recent history to link homosexuality with child molestation. In *The Sexual Victimization of Children*, de Young recalls the campaign and notes the ways in which Bryant successfully exploited "every parent's nightmare" — the deeply rooted fear that homosexuals "recruit" because they "cannot have children." De Young comments,

> The subtle shading of the practice of homosexuality between consenting adults into homosexual as- saults on children did not go unnoticed by many researchers who had found the latter connection spurious at best. Even the best attempts at educat- ing the public to the realities of homosexuality and child molestation had difficulty in penetrating the homophobia and the "compassionate and sympa- thetic" hostility of people who, often for the first time, were giving serious consideration to ... "the largest American minority" [i.e., gay men and lesbians] ....

> While few would argue that child molestation is indeed every parent's nightmare, there is actually a comparatively less reason to fear homosexual assaults on children than most people believe. Researchers have variously estimated its occurrence at 19 percent of reported molestations, 25 percent, and 33 percent. Even at its maximum proposed rate of 33 percent, from a purely statistical point of view and relying on reported cases, it is clear that a child is much more likely to be heterosexually than homosexually mo- lested.[111] (Citations omitted.)

---

[111] de Young, M. (1982). *The sexual victimization of children*. Jefferson, NC: McFarland & Co., Inc., p. 142.

Nicholas Groth and his research group at the Connecticut Correctional Institute, in addition, are among the country's foremost experts on sexual offenses against children. They have repeatedly noted the lack of a connection between homosexuality and child molestation.[112] For example, they point out:

> [T]he belief that homosexuals are particularly attracted to children is completely unsupported by our data. The child offenders who engaged in adult sexual relations as well were heterosexual. Those offenders who selected underage male victims either have always done so or have regressed from adult *heterosexual* relations. These were no homosexual, adult-oriented offenders in our sample who turned to children.[113] (Emphasis in original.)

Finally, in their landmark, decade-long study of the development of sexual preference, Bell, Weinberg, and Hammersmith noted that, of their male and female homosexual respondents who had engaged in childhood or adolescent same-sex sexual behavior, the overwhelming majority experienced such sex play with friends and age-mates, not with strangers and adults.[114]

Interestingly, a small minority of *both* heterosexual and homosexual respondents had experienced homosexual sex with someone significantly older or with an adult while they were children or adolescents. The heterosexual respondents, however, obviously continued to develop heterosexually. In the authors' "path

---

[112]   Groth, A. N. (1978). Patterns of sexual assault against children and adolescents. In A. W. Burgess, A. N. Groth, L. L. Holmstrom, & S. M. Sgroi (Eds.), *Sexual assault of children and adolescents* (pp. 3-24). Lexington, MA: Lexington Books. *See also* Groth, A. N. & Birnbaum, H. J. (1978). Adult sexual orientation and attraction to underage persons. *Archives of Sexual Behavior, 7*(3), 175-181.

[113]   Groth, *supra*, pp. 4-5.

[114]   Bell, A. P., Weinberg, M. S., & Hammersmith, S. K. (1981). *Sexual preference: Its development in men and women.* Bloomington, IN: Indiana University Press.

analysis" concept of factors that accounted for, and led to, the development of adult sexual preference, they accorded no value whatsoever to childhood or adolescent contact with same-sex adults.

This same point is made by Lehne, whose own research revealed that

> only 4 percent of the male homosexuals [surveyed] reported that they were somewhat seduced into their first homosexual act, and in no case was force involved. By contrast, Sorensen reports that the first sexual experience of 6 percent of nonvirgin adolescent girls was heterosexual rape.[115]

Tindall, too, covered this ground in his longitudinal study of nine boys who experienced homosexual pederastic relationships in adolescence.[116] Even into the fourth decade after these experiences, none of the nine respondents had become homosexual in his adult life.

Although there is every reason to be concerned about the problem of child sexual abuse in America, it is clear that the greatest potential threat to children comes from heterosexual males, not from lesbians and gay men. One imagines that reasonable men and women, after educating themselves as to the relevant facts, would find reason to discard beliefs in the propensity of homosexuals to assault children sexually.

Stigma

The stigma that is presumed to attach to children of lesbian or gay parents is another of the common objections to parenting by homosexuals. Polikoff explains that

---

[115] Lehne, G. K. (1976). Homophobia among men. In D. S. David & R. Brannon, (Eds.), *The forty-nine percent majority: The male sex role* (pp. 66-88). Reading, MA: Addison-Wesley Pub. Co., p. 75. Citing Sorenson, R. (1973). *Adolescent sexuality in contemporary America.* NY: World.

[116] Tindall, R. (1978). The male adolescent involved with a pederast becomes an adult. *Journal of Homosexuality, 3*(4), 373-382.

[c]hildren and teenagers often face [a variety of pressures to conform].... The price of failure to conform can be ostracism or harassment. A child can be denied access to a desired friendship circle for being too smart or too dumb, too obedient or too rebellious. Wearing glasses, being overweight, or having big ears can subject a child to disturbing taunts....

Children whose families are in some way different from the norm may have to confront distressing reactions from others. These differences can include, among other things, the family's ethnic traits and practices, race, religious affiliation, the parent's country of origin, physical appearance, or occupation. Children are understandably disturbed by hearing their schoolmates say, "Your mom's a fatty!" or "Hey, Jew boy, where are your horns?" or by being rejected because they are black or because their father is a mortician.[117]

Child-placement decisions based on the presumption of stigma and harassment, however, embody two significant errors. First, there is reason to believe that the impact on children of a parent's homosexuality has been grossly exaggerated by those opposed to lesbian and gay parenting. (This issue is discussed in detail in Chapter Six.) In summary, it is sufficient to say that children of lesbian and gay parents simply do not report incidents of harassment and abuse to an extent that justifies a belief that this is their inevitable fate. Nor, as reports of their psychological health demonstrate, do they apparently suffer crippling stigma or ostracism.

Second, as others have commented, ostracism of a child because she or he has a lesbian or gay parent can no longer take place if prejudice based on sexual orientation is eliminated. Indeed, fostering respect for diversity and eliminating prejudice against gay men and lesbians can be seen as an important task for

---

[117] Polikoff, *supra*, pp. 567-568.

social welfare organizations, schools, churches, government, and, indeed, for society itself. These same institutions have, in fact, set themselves the goal of rectifying other kinds of social prejudice, such as that based on race, physical handicap, gender, and so forth.

We do not, for example, commonly suggest that Blacks or Asians or women or the disabled remain in hiding to avoid offending the sensibilities of others. We do not create laws and policies that prohibit mixed-race couples from raising children because of the stigma that may befall them (although America once did precisely that). And, if the shy child or the overweight child or the child with a limp is ridiculed on the playground, we don't throw up our hands and tell the unhappy victim, "Too bad, that's what you get for being the way you are."

There is, moreover, a great tradition in the helping professions of providing empathy, guidance, and advocacy to those who must attempt to "fit into" a world intolerant of diversity. Consider some of the many books available to parents of children with disabilities;[118] to children in families involved in divorce or marital separation;[119] to daughters whose fathers have died, committed suicide, or abandoned the family;[120] to families with dwarf children;[121] or to disillusioned working-class white families facing the decline of "traditional" values.[122]

The problems of children growing up Black, Chicano, Nisei, Filipino, Chinese, or as members of numerous other ethnic groups in white America are likewise explored in myriad forums, as are

---

[118] Miezio, P. M. (1983). *Parenting children with disabilities: A professional source for physicians and a guide for parents.* Levittown, PA: The Phoenix Society.

[119] Stuart, I. & Abt, L. (Eds.) (1981). *Children of separation and divorce: Management and treatment.* New York: Van Nostrand Reinhold.

[120] Wakerman, E. (1984). Father loss: *Daughters discuss the man that got away.* NY: Doubleday.

[121] Ablon, J. (1988). *Living with difference: Families with dwarf children.* NY: Praeger.

[122] Rubin, L. R. (1976). *Worlds of pain: Life in the working-class family.* NY: Basic Books.

issues related to coping with an alcoholic or abusive family. The salient feature is this: In no case is the suggestion made that "different" children and their families *deserve* stigma or that they must shoulder all responsibility for either avoiding or adapting to prejudice. In no case, that is, except with regard to the children of lesbian or gay parents.

In analyzing the trauma that many commentators are convinced is the destiny of the child of the lesbian or gay family, Ricketts and Achtenberg suggest that an apparent concern for the welfare of children actually conceals an

> insistence that children be sheltered from every experience in which their difference might challenge prejudice, ignorance, or the status quo (or in which they would be "exposed" to the difference of others). Agencies conforming to such a standard must ask themselves whether it is their function to honor the system that generates stigma by upholding its constraints.[123]

In effect, if agencies refuse to place children with lesbian or gay foster parents on the basis of the "possible trauma" argument, they are perpetuating the prejudices of society. Perhaps more pointedly, foster care agencies must decide what situation is more likely to traumatize a child — a life of multiple placements, institutional care, or temporary group shelters, or life in a private home with qualified lesbian or gay foster parents.

Tom Herman and his lover, Jeremy, a New Hampshire couple of 15 years' standing, had been foster parents for over a decade when their state outlawed lesbian and gay foster homes (see Chapter Six). During the controversy created by the new law, the couple and their teenage foster son, Jody, who is heterosexual, were featured in the 1987 TV documentary, "We Are Family," produced by Aimee Sands and WGBH-TV/Boston.

---

[123]   Ricketts & Achtenberg, 1990, *supra*, p. 89.

Because of continuous trouble with the law, Jody had been in and out of juvenile hall and jails for most of his adolescence. Now 22, Jody went to live with Tom and Jeremy after he had "used up" all other possible placements. In "We Are Family," Jody discusses what it was like to move in with two men known openly in their community as gay. Rather than be wary of Tom and Jeremy because they were gay, Jody says, he was concerned that "they could have been prejudiced against people who had been in jail or in trouble with the law."

Tom Herman later commented:

> Jody came to us as sort of an outcast. He'd been labeled and branded as someone who was on the wrong side of the law. And we know a lot of different kinds of people, we're very integrated into the community, and Jody used to get a kick out of the fact that wherever we would go, a lot of people would know us and come up and hug   us — people of all different lifestyles. I've known his probation officer for 15 years, for example; there were people who are counselors in his school who were my students when I was teaching graduate school. So he got to experience being proud of being in our family.

> People often say that it isn't "fair" to bring a "troubled" child into a home where there're gay parents — but what's fair about a child who is otherwise likely to live in an environment that's completely devoid of emotional and psychological support? You're dealing with kids who are starved for consistency, security, and love.

> I get irate when people talk about eliminating placements on the basis of sexual preference. How truly little that has to do with the environment a child needs if he's going to undo some of the stress and the hurt that has gotten him into the situation he's in!

I hope I will see, in my lifetime, a time when people
are scrutinized on the basis of whether they have
the skills to get themselves through very trying
times to create placements for these kids, and on
the basis of their ability to be open and available.
The last thing that's an issue is lifestyle, and the
first thing that should be an issue is competency.[124]

The Child Welfare Worker's Professional Responsibilities

Finally, it is important to note that the American Psychological
Association, the American Psychiatric Association, and the National Association of Social Workers have all adopted official
policy statements that explicitly address the placement of foster
children with lesbians or gay men. These statements are included
in Appendix C. In all cases, the ethical responsibility and policy-
setting committees for the respective professions have examined
the issues and have spoken out against discrimination against
lesbian and gay foster parents. Helping professionals are bound
by these policies. If a child welfare worker is compelled by state
law or social service regulations to exclude prospective foster
parents on the sole basis of their sexual orientation — and therefore must violate professional codes of conduct — support may be
available to the worker through her or his professional
assembly.

---

[124] Tom Herman, personal communication, August 4, 1988.

CHAPTER FIVE

The Boston Foster Care Case [125]

One of the most dramatic examples of "official" responses to gay and lesbian foster parenting involved the case of a Massachusetts gay couple named David Jean and Donald Babets. In early 1984, the two men applied to the Department of Social Services in Boston to be licensed as foster parents. In some ways, Babets and Jean were more stable, upstanding, and financially secure than many individuals who apply for licensure in Massachusetts and across the country: Babets was a senior investigator for the Boston Fair Housing Commission and Jean was the business manager of a nursing home. Actively involved in community affairs and in local electoral politics, the men brought with them enthusiastic letters of reference from Babets' priest and Jean's minister.

Babets and Jean, however, had decided to submit their application openly as a gay couple. After living together as domestic partners for more than a decade, the men felt that it was better to enter the situation candidly than to risk the possibility that the nature of their relationship would be "discovered" later — to their detriment.

Slightly more than a year later, after an evaluation period twice as long as that for most prospective foster parents and a particularly extensive round of home visits, interviews, and investigations of the men's reputations on the job and in the community, the Massachusetts DSS approved Babets and Jean's

---

[125] The research behind this account of the Boston Foster Care case was conducted for publication in Ricketts & Achtenberg, 1987, *supra*. Some of the material used here has also appeared elsewhere in different form.

joint application and granted them a license. A short time later, two little boys — ages 3 and nearly 2 — were placed in the Babets and Jean home. The boys' mother had given written approval for the placement.

On May 8, 1985, less than two weeks after the children were placed with Babets and Jean, the *Boston Globe* broke the story of the placement on the front page of its "Metro" section. "Some Oppose Foster Placement With Gay Couple," the headline read.[126]

It remains unclear how the *Globe* first learned that the children had been placed with Babets and Jean. Some believe that a neighbor phoned the newspaper to complain; others maintain that the information was "leaked" to the *Globe* from within the Department of Social Services and that the *Globe* then launched its own investigation. Whichever version is accurate, it is clear that the *Globe* had, from the beginning, known the identities of the parties involved.

Although the *Globe's* May 8th story did not identify Babets and Jean by name, Kenneth Cooper, the reporter who prepared the story and who continued to write follow-up articles for several months, acknowledged that he had interviewed Donald Babets before the initial piece ran. He recalled, "Babets suggested to me that if I did the story the kids could be taken out of the home. I wasn't persuaded of that. He was."[127]

It was also apparent, from quotes in the *Globe's* May 8th story, that Cooper (or other *Globe* reporters) informed Babets and Jean's neighbors and various Roxbury community leaders about the placement and solicited their reactions.

The *Globe's* initial coverage created a flurry of activity within the DSS. On the morning of the day the story appeared, Commissioner of Social Services Marie Matava personally assured Babets

---

[126]   Cooper, K. J. (1985, May 8). Some oppose foster placement with gay couple. *Boston Globe*, 21, 24.

[127]   Kenneth J. Cooper, personal communication, July 29, 1986.

and Jean that the children would not be taken from their home.[128] But by the afternoon, as reporters and TV cameras descended on the scene, DSS officials abruptly removed the two boys. A statement issued by the Department blamed the "public controversy" surrounding the placement as the impetus behind the DSS's decision to move the boys.[129]

As the situation developed, the *Globe* remained a powerful influence, and stories on the placement and related issues ran almost daily for weeks. The editors' opinion of foster placements with lesbians and gay men was also expressed repeatedly in a series of editorials. The first, which appeared only five days after the removal of the children, appeared to be an early attempt at a more-or-less moderate position and included this rather curious analysis:

> The goal of foster care is to remove a child from an abnormal home setting and place him in as normal a home setting as possible.... If the foster children are below school age, the setting will be most normal if the woman stays home as a full-time caretaker.... Applying that test to the [Babets and Jean case], the two homosexual men would have been rejected as foster parents not because of their sexual preference, but because of the deviation of their household — consisting of two working men — from the normal setting sought as foster-care placement for pre-school children.[130]

The next two weeks, however, brought furious organizing on the part of both opponents and advocates of lesbian and gay foster parenting. The *Globe's* editorial pages were full of letters criticizing the paper's concept of the "normal home"; and, in the

---

[128]   Kevin J. Cathcart, attorney for Babets and Jean, personal communication, July 7, 1986.

[129]   Cooper, K. J. (1985, May 9). Placement of foster children with gay couple is revoked. *Boston Globe*, 1, 9.

[130]   A normal home setting. (1985, May 13). *Boston Globe*.

community, the *Globe* was caught in the cross-fire between opposing factions — many of whom agreed only in condemning the
media.

It was also true, in the time between the *Globe's* May 13th and
May 28th editorials, that critics of the DSS's decision and of the
Globe's editorial position managed to wage an effective public
campaign of their own, and the newspaper found itself on something of a limb in opposing "nontraditional" placements in general and gay homes in particular. Perhaps in response to these
issues, the *Globe* quickly began to take a much less moderate
position on gay and lesbian foster parents — one that actually
seemed more concordant with the tone of its reportage. On May
28th the editors wrote:

> The state's foster-care program is not a place for
> experimentation with nontraditional family set-
> tings. It should never be used, knowingly or
> unknowingly, as the means by which homosexuals
> who do not have children of their own...are en-
> abled to acquire the trappings of traditional fami-
> lies. Despite the contentions of homosexuals and of
> single working women that they can be loving and
> caring with children, the needs of the troubled
> children who must be removed from their natural
> homes and placed in foster care are best met in
> family settings that are stable and free from social
> stress. [131]

When the two children were taken from the Babets and Jean
home, it was not immediately clear who had ordered their removal. Anonymous sources quoted in the gay and lesbian press
alleged that Governor Michael Dukakis had personally ordered
the placement to be changed as soon as the story appeared in the
Globe.

Official claims, however, were that the decision had been
made at a lower level and was motivated by concern over the

---

[131]   A model foster-care policy. (1985, May 28). *Boston Globe*, 14.

negative effects of publicity on the children and not by embarrassment over the licensing of a gay couple. Governor Dukakis, meanwhile, told reporters that he was unaware that the state was making gay foster placements,[132] a position he adopted as soon as the Babets and Jean story broke and which he maintained throughout the case. The Governor's assertion, however, appears not to have been wholly true.

As early as 1976, that is, Dukakis received a report on foster care from a Department of Public Welfare Study that he had commissioned. The Summary of the Project's final report stated, in part,

> [T]he results of the review in this category do not indicate that alleged or professed homosexuality, per se, is evidence of unsuitability as a foster parent. Rather, greater cause for concern was found in the issue of supporting and assisting workers in dealing with cases that may involve single (male) parents and/or homosexuality.[133]

The report, which was made public, was the subject of an article in a national gay newspaper, *The Advocate*, in which the report's author, Assistant Welfare Commissioner Beth Warren, discussed the cooperation of the Boston Gay Community in the preparation of the report.[134] Foster placements, that is, had all along been taking place with lesbians and gay men and were no secret.

Like Dukakis, Commissioner Matava denied that she had been aware of the Babets and Jean placement. The *Globe*, however, quoted a DSS spokesperson as saying that, although the DSS didn't question prospective foster parents about their sexual

---

[132] Cooper, K. J. (1985, May 25). New policy on foster care: Parenting by gays all but ruled out. *Boston Globe*, 1, 24, p. 24.

[133] Warden, B. (1976, March 3). *Summary of report: Administrative case review of foster care placements.* Boston, MA: Commonwealth of Massachusetts, Department of Public Welfare, p. 3.

[134] No evidence gay parents unsuitable. (1976, April 21). *The Advocate*, 12-13.

preference, "[I]f the sexual preference issue comes up during the screening process, the case is referred to and reviewed by the central office."[135] Babets told the *Globe* that notification of the couple's approval as foster parents had come personally from Deputy Commissioner Joseph Collins.[136] Given the length and intensity of the investigation to which Babets and Jean were subjected, and the fact that the DSS admitted that Babets and Jean's was the first license granted to a gay couple, it seems unlikely that Matava could have been unaware of the placement.

Whether or not Dukakis and Matava knew about Babets and Jean or other lesbian and gay foster placements, Dukakis was personally responsible for ordering the DSS immediately "to produce a policy on the placement of foster children in gay households," a development reported by the *Globe*.[137] The *Globe* was, in fact, at least partly responsible for manufacturing the "separate policy" issue, and its first two articles on the Babets and Jean case devoted considerable space to "exposing" the DSS's lack of a policy. In both articles, Cooper repeated the same quote from Commissioner Matava — "We can't discriminate based on anything"— but presented it in such a way that Matava appeared to be conceding that the DSS had only minimal standards for foster parents.[138] On May 13th, the *Globe* editorialized:

> The most troubling aspect of the state's decision to approve two homosexual men as foster parents is that the state did so after extensive discussion of the particular case but without the guidance of an overall policy on the placement of foster children in nontraditional households.[139]

---

[135] Cooper, May 8, 1985, *supra*, p. 24.

[136] Cooper, May 9, 1985, *supra*, p. 1.

[137] Cooper, K. J. (1985, May 10). Policy sought on placements in gay homes. *Boston Globe*, 1, 9.

[138] Cooper, May 9, 1985, *supra*, p. 9; Cooper, May 10, 1985, *supra*, p.9.

[139] A normal home setting, *supra*.

If the *Globe's* intention was to embarrass the DSS and the Governor because of the absence of a separate policy governing lesbian and gay foster placements, it succeeded. Like most states, it was true, Massachusetts's foster care policy made no specific mention of gay or lesbian applicants. But Governor Dukakis and the DSS immediately accepted the *Globe's* inference — that the absence of a specific policy (particularly an exclusionary one) was evidence of negligence. Rather than affirm that Babets and Jean had more than adequately fulfilled all DSS protocols, Dukakis ordered the DSS to write a new policy. As Babets and Jean's attorney, Kevin Cathcart, noted:

> The DSS looked foolish because they didn't seem to have a policy to cover gay people. Instead of saying, "Yes, we have a policy and Jean and Babets fit!" they set out to write a new and separate policy.[140]

Indeed, in May, 1985 the Massachusetts Executive Office of Human Services conducted a survey of 47 states, including the District of Columbia, regarding the status of lesbian and gay foster parents.[141] The EOHS research revealed that 41 states had no specific "official" policy governing lesbian and gay foster care placements, and that four states had favorable policies. Only two states "officially" prohibited lesbian and gay foster parents: Florida, which had also outlawed lesbian and gay adoptions in 1977, and North Dakota, which required foster parents to be married.

Citing a variety of "unofficial" policies, however, 13 additional states indicated that they would *not* place children in a gay foster home.[142] Of the 17 states that stated they had placed and would

---

[140] Personal communication, July 7, 1986.

[141] Review of states' policies regarding foster placements. (1985, May). Commonwealth of Massachusetts, Executive Office of Human Services.

[142] Many of these same states acknowledged, however, that lesbian or gay foster placements may have taken place without their knowledge, since they did not assess the sexual orientation of prospective foster parents.

continue to place foster children in gay households, most cited their policy against sexual orientation discrimination and added that applicants' sexual preference was not asked. Fifteen other states maintained that they had never faced the issue officially.

Notably, the question of "official" vs. "unofficial" policies made an accurate summary of states' rules difficult. When the *Globe* attempted its own informal survey, its results differed somewhat from the information gathered by EOHS personnel. The *Globe*, for example, reported: "In Illinois, singles may be foster parents, but unmarrieds living in the same household — whether heterosexual or homosexual — may not" and "Like Massachusetts, Florida has no policy."[143]

In contrast, the Massachusetts EOHS survey reported that Florida had a policy prohibiting lesbian or gay placements (actually a state law), and that Illinois had "a strong feeling that the state cannot discriminate against gays," even though it had no policy. These examples illustrate the difficulty of accurately ascertaining states' actual practices regarding lesbian and gay foster homes. Perhaps even more, they reflect the reluctance of state spokespeople to commit themselves to an "official" position on this issue.

As the Massachusetts DSS continued its own efforts to develop an official policy, at least part of its motivation was an awareness of public and media scrutiny. Secretary of Human Services Philip Johnston would later say,

> I was startled to find the same kind of uncertainty and confusion exists in most other states regarding this issue. So I think other states are going to be looking to us to set some kind of national standard.[144]

Babets and Jean, meanwhile, retained an attorney and began to pursue the administrative and legal options available to them, even as debate on lesbian and gay foster parenting began in the

---

[143] Longcope, K. (1985, May 12). States' policies differ on issue of gay foster parents. *Boston Globe*, 23.

[144] Cooper, May 25, 1985, *supra,*. p. 24.

Massachusetts legislature. As early as May 14th, a resolution was offered in the House that directed the DSS to "place children in need of foster care exclusively in the care of those persons whose sexual orientation presents no threat to the well-being of the child."[145]

Slightly more than a week later, an even more strongly worded ban on gay and lesbian foster parents (as well as in adoption, guardianship, family day care, and respite care) passed the House by a vote of 112-28.[146] Outside the State House, several hundred people protested on the Boston Common. The very next day, on May 24, 1985, Secretary Johnston announced the Commonwealth's new policy for foster care placements. The policy, codified as Commonwealth of Massachusetts Regulations 110 (CMR) 7.101, stated:

> *7.101: Placement with Relatives, Others*
>
> ...
>
> The Department shall consider the following placement resources in the following order:
>
> (g) placement in the child's own home;
>
> (h) placement in family foster care with relatives, with consideration given to extended family members and persons chosen by the parent(s) for substitute care;
>
> (i) placement in family foster care with a married couple preferably with parenting experience and time available for parenting;
>
> (j) placement in family foster care with a person with parenting experience and preferably with time available for parenting;

---

[145] Cooper, K. J. (1985, May 16). Officials check other states' policies on foster care. *Boston Globe*, 15.

[146] Cooper, K. J. (1985, May 24). House votes to ban gay foster parents. *Boston Globe*, 1, 24.

(k)   placement in family foster care with a person without parenting experience and preferably with time available for parenting;

(l)   placement in community residential care.

Any placement made pursuant to 110 CMR 7.101(1)(j) or (k) shall require the written approval of the Commissioner.

Although it did not mention the words "gay" or "lesbian," the new policy created a hierarchy under which "non-traditional" placements were to receive consideration only if "it can be clearly demonstrated that there is no traditional family setting available, or likely to be available, for the child in question."[147]

The preferred settings, as outlined in the policy, meant (1) relatives of the child or married couples with parenting experience and (2) married couples without parenting experience. The new regulations required the Department to place children with foster parents in the first two categories before even considering unmarried couples or single parents, including gay and lesbian couples or singles, and made placements in these "third-tier" settings impossible without the express written approval of the Commissioner of Social Services. In addition, all future licensing applications were to include a question that asked the prospective foster parent's sexual orientation.

At the press conference announcing the new policy, Secretary of Human Services Johnston admitted that future placements with gay and lesbian foster parents were "highly unlikely" and stated that Babets and Jean "'would not have been approved as foster parents' under the new policy."[148]

Outcry against the new policy began almost immediately at sit-ins, protest rallies, public hearings, and at a statewide professional conference of mental health and children/youth organizations. The July, 1985 newsletter of the Service Employees'

---

[147]   Cooper, May 25, 1985, *supra*, p. 24.

[148]   Cooper, May 25, 1985, *supra*, pp. 1, 24.

International Union Local 509 noted that the new regulations would make social workers' jobs more difficult, and included comments from an anonymous Boston DSS worker who called herself "Marion."

Disputing the DSS's contention that Massachusetts had "more foster homes than children needed foster care," Marion cited her years of experience in the field and noted,

> As usual, DSS and other foster care workers are expected to implement a misguided policy. We keep wondering — what will the impact be?...It seems as if political decision-making is replacing clinical judgment and common sense.[149]

The Commonwealth's mental health experts, social workers, and child welfare professionals, it is clear, were virtually united in opposition to the new policy. On June 21st, the Massachusetts Association for Mental Health and four other groups sponsored a "Forum on Foster Care Placements and the Placement of Children with Gay Parents." Representatives from 41 agencies and associations testified at the public event. Not one of them supported the new foster care policy.

The Civil Liberties Union of Massachusetts' newsletter noted,

> Virtually everyone stressed that children's needs are best served by making foster care selections on a case-by-case basis without excluding any particular group. The unanimous theme of the testimony was that gay men, lesbians, and singles can be good, caring parents and there is no valid reason to exclude them. Rarely is there such agreement in the human services field.[150]

---

[149] Coleman, J., Phillips, S. & Waldfogel, J. (1985, July). New foster care policy means DSS workers' jobs harder. *509 News.*

[150] Law suit to challenge DSS foster child placement policy. (1985, August). *The Docket,* 15(3).

In fact, despite this massive opposition effort by individuals (including Gloria Steinem and Geraldine Ferraro), by state politicians (such as State Attorney General Frank X. Bellotti and a dozen of the Commonwealth's senators and representatives), by the newly formed Gay and Lesbian Defense Committee, and by representatives of virtually every human service organization and agency in Massachusetts — including the National Association of Social Workers, the Massachusetts Human Services Coalition, the National Lawyers Guild, the Northeast Council of Child Protection, the Massachusetts Society for the Prevention of Cruelty to Children, the Rainbow Coalition, Boston Children's Services, the Civil Liberties Union of Massachusetts, and the Massachusetts Psychiatric Society, to name a few — the new regulations were approved. By August, Deputy Commissioner Joseph Collins had resigned in protest, an action he had wanted to take in May, but delayed at the request of Commissioner Matava.

In December of 1985, the Massachusetts Committee for Children and Youth sponsored a "Speakout on Foster Care," a forum for legislators, policy makers, and child welfare workers to discuss problems in the Massachusetts foster care system. In its report on the Speakout, the Committee noted that the new foster care policy,

> [which placed] priority on placement in traditional
> two parent foster families, discourage[d] placement
> with single parents and virtually eliminat[ed] gay
> foster parents from among placement possibilities,
> has exacerbated many of the problems listed
> [herein], particularly recruitment. It... excludes
> many competent, nurturing people from among the
> pool of foster parent resources.[151]

Nonetheless, one year after the incident that began the Babets and Jean case, the *Boston Globe* marked the anniversary with a congratulatory editorial. The *Globe's* editors wrote:

---

[151] Massachusetts Committee for Children and Youth. (1985, December 18). *Summary of proceedings of the speakout on foster care.* Boston, MA: Author, p. 6.

One year ago, the Department of Social Services
removed two young boys from the home of the two
homosexual men who were serving as their foster
parents. As difficult as it might have been to
envision then, the incident has produced major
benefits for foster children.[152]

Among the "benefits" perceived by the *Globe* were a new
emphasis on what it called "normal" families — in which the
husband was employed and the wife stayed home to care for the
children. Although the *Globe's* editorial reported that the Commonwealth had, with concerted effort, been able to recruit an
additional 250 "traditional" couples in the first four months of
1986 and implied that all Massachusetts' foster children were thus
all currently housed in private-home placements, a December,
1985 report by the Commonwealth's Legislative Subcommittee on
Foster Care told a different story.

The Legislative Subcommittee noted that 50 to 58 percent of
state and private placement agencies maintained significant
waiting lists, and estimated that, at the time of its publication, as
many as 750 children were awaiting foster care in inappropriate or
emergency settings.[153] In May, 1985, in fact, Commissioner
Matava herself had indicated that Massachusetts was in need of 25
percent more homes to serve its 6,500 foster children.[154]

---

[152] Foster-Care lessons. (1986, May 11). *Boston Globe.*

[153] Hildt, B., Kollios, P., Parente, M. & Buell, C. (1985, December). *In the best
interest of the children?* Boston, MA: Commonwealth of Massachusetts Joint
Committee on Human Services and Elderly Affairs, Legislative Subcommittee on Foster Care.

[154] Cooper, May 10, 1985, *supra*, p. 9. Even making the unlikely assumption that
Massachusetts could have placed three children in each of its then-existing
foster homes, Matava's estimate meant that the Commonwealth was some
540 foster families short of its goal. At the time, in fact, Massachusetts
maintained 4,737 foster homes. Calculated another way, then, 1,184 more
placements were needed to meet the 25% shortfall that Matava spoke of —
far more than the 250 homes the *Globe* believed had been sufficient to put an
end to waiting by Massachusetts' foster children.

In its official statements, however, the Massachusetts DSS continued to dispute the Hildt, et al. findings and to insist that a shortage of foster homes would not result from a change in the placement policy. Yet only three weeks after the DSS banned gay, lesbian, and other "non-traditional" homes, the *Globe* reported,

> The Massachusetts Department of Social Services, frustrated in past efforts to recruit more foster parents, has undertaken a campaign aimed at relieving the chronic shortage of temporary guardians for troubled children in state custody.[155]

The article went on to note that new recruitment efforts entailed the hiring of a private marketing firm to find potential foster parents; a massive public campaign, including "notes on milk cartons and in utility bills...announcements at Red Sox games, and cable television programs,"[156] and the establishment of a toll-free "800" number. The impact anticipated by "Marion" in her union's newsletter, in other words, was beginning to make itself felt.

The Litigation

In January of 1986, after an Administrative Appeal process had failed, Donald Babets and David Jean joined a number of other plaintiffs and brought suit against Governor Dukakis and the DSS. They alleged that the priority system established by the promulgation of the new foster care policy

> create[d] an arbitrary and irrational presumption that all unmarried couples and single persons, even those with parenting experience, are always less suitable as foster parents than are married couples (even those without parenting experience).[157]

---

[155] Cooper, K. J. (1985, June 10). State trying to find more foster parents. *Boston Globe*, 21, 24, p. 24.

[156] *Ibid.*

[157] Complaint of Donald L. Babets, David H. Jean, et al., filed January 30, 1986 in the Superior Court Department of the Trial Court of the Commonwealth, Suffolk County, Massachusetts, p. 8.

In addition, the Complaint challenged the new requirement that prospective foster parents divulge their sexual orientation on the DSS screening form. One of the Plaintiffs, the Reverend Kathryn Piccard, had been a foster parent for 6 years. During that time, 17 children had been placed with her. She was removed from the list of licensed parents, however, when she refused to answer the sexual orientation question prior to being approved for an eighteenth placement.

The Plaintiffs further charged that the intent of the state's new regulation was to create an "arbitrary, invidiously discriminatory, and unreasonable classification of foster parents" based on sexual orientation.[158] The new regulation made state policy of the presumption that unmarried or homosexual individuals were *per se* unfit to be foster parents, the Plaintiffs argued. The DSS, they went on, was prohibited by law from rejecting foster parents on the basis of such an arbitrary classification, particularly in the absence of any rational basis for the presumption (e.g., scientific evidence) and without a demonstration that the distinction served or protected an important purpose of government. Almost immediately, the state moved to have the lawsuit dismissed, alleging that none of the Plaintiffs' legal claims was valid.

In September of 1986, Judge Thomas R. Morse, Jr. ruled on the Defendants' Motion to Dismiss, upholding the most important of Plaintiffs' allegations.[159] Judge Morse's ruling, however, was only an opinion on the validity — as a matter of law, not as a matter of fact — of the Plaintiffs' complaint. That is, he determined whether or not the Plaintiffs had a valid legal complaint, assuming they could prove all the facts they alleged. The issues of fact — for instance, whether or not it was actually true that the State intended to discriminate against unmarried people and homosexuals — were left to be decided when all the evidence was presented at trial.

---

[158] *Ibid.*, p. 12.

[159] Morse, Hon. Samuel J. (1986) . Memorandum and order on defendants' motion to dismiss . Commonwealth of Massachusetts Superior Court Action No. 81083.

First, Judge Morse upheld the claim that the creation of an arbitrary classification, on the basis of which some individuals were prevented from becoming foster parents, violated the Plaintiffs' rights to equal protection under both the Massachusetts and U. S. Constitutions. The guarantee of equal protection of the laws "is essentially a direction that all persons similarly situated should be treated alike."[160] The court noted: "If the best interests of the child are to govern all out of home foster placements ... then any distinction between married couples and single persons is wholly arbitrary and capricious and adverse to the needs of children."[161]

As Judge Morse noted in his Order, and as Plaintiffs intended to emphasize at trial, the Babets and Jean home had been carefully and systematically examined by the DSS before the men were licensed as foster parents and children were placed with them. In the two weeks between the placement and the removal of the children, the couple did nothing to warrant the revocation of the placement and the DSS discovered no new information which showed that parenting by homosexuals was detrimental to children. In light of that, the State's reliance on no new facts to support the termination of a placement it had previously approved revealed that the new foster care policy was arbitrary on its face. Judge Morse concluded:

> Any exclusion of homosexuals from consideration as foster parents, all things being equal, is blatantly irrational.... Plaintiffs are entitled to prove that discrimination based on sexual preference stems from the defendants' 'bare desire to harm a politically unpopular group,' and that it is not a legitimate state interest.[162]

---

[160] *Ibid.*, p. 10.

[161] *Ibid.*, p. 13.

[162] *Ibid.*, pp. 15-16.

In early 1987, a Special Commission on Foster Care, appointed by Governor Dukakis in Spring of 1986, issued its "Final Recommendations" regarding modifications that it believed were needed in the Massachusetts foster care system. The Commis-sion's report, which represented months of study and delved broadly into all areas of foster care, including reimbursements to foster parents, medical care, clothing allowances for teenaged children, and interracial placements, also suggested the elimination of the placement hierarchy that had been established in May of 1985. The report stated,

> Once the decision is made to place a child outside of his or her home, the Commonwealth must first look at the following placement resources, in order of priority: 1. Other members of the child's imme-diate family; 2. Members of the child's extended family; 3.Foster homes that reflect the child's cultural, religious, racial, ethnic, and community identities.... In selecting a foster home, the Com-monwealth must consider a number of factors, including the age, race, ethnic background, reli-gion, sex, sexual preference, marital status, eco-nomic status, employment status, geographic location, or education of the potential foster parent. None of these factors should be an overriding determinant in a person's eligibility to become a foster parent.... Again, the ultimate standard in each case must be, Can this foster home provide a temporary, stable, nurturing environment for this child? This decision can only be made on a case-by-case basis.... The decision of when and where to place an individual child should be made at the area level by the staff who are closest to the case and best able to assess the individual placement needs of the child...."[163]

---

[163] Legal and Policy Issues: Recommendation 5 — Placement Policy, pp. 28-29. In *EOHS Special Commission on Foster Care: Final Recommendations.* (1989, December 17). Boston, MA: Executive Office of Human Services.

Governor Dukakis accepted the majority of the Commission's recommendations. He did not, however, accept the call for a change in the DSS placement policy vis-a-vis gay men and lesbians, or in the presumption that sexual orientation was determinative of fitness. No known lesbians or gay men were subsequently approved as new foster parents and, as attorney Kevin Cathcart explained in early 1988,

> There are lesbian and gay foster parents on the
> DSS's [former] "approved" list who have had no
> placements made with them for almost 3 years.
> The same is true with foster parents who refused to
> answer the sexual orientation question. Those the
> state sees as of "indeterminate" orientation, and
> they do not receive foster placements.[164]

Cathcart also noted that information received by his office indicated that the DSS had stopped requiring single, heterosexual foster parent applicants to be reviewed separately by the DSS Commissioner. "If that is true," Cathcart noted,

> it proves our contention that this whole process
> was set up as a way of weeding out lesbian and gay
> foster parents, and that the requirement for sign-off
> for all single parents was basically a smokescreen.
> We always maintained that the sign-off would be
> automatic for heterosexual single parents; in fact, it
> appears to have become so automatic that they
> have dispensed with it as a waste of time and
> paperwork.[165]

After that time, Plaintiffs did further battle with the Commonwealth over the release of various documents that they believed would demonstrate that the DSS had developed and enacted the new foster care policy in an "arbitrary, unreasonable, and discriminatory" fashion. Massachusetts' attorneys claimed that

---

[164] Personal communication, February 26, 1988.

[165] *Ibid.*

governmental privilege shielded the DSS from any sort of public scrutiny about the way in which it created policies. Noted Cathcart,

> [T]he governor claimed his policy was based upon sound recommendations from child welfare experts. In reality the experts disagreed with him. The governor did not want memos pertaining to the formulation of the policy made public and claimed "executive privilege" when we requested them in the course of our suit.[166]

In August, 1988, Justices of Massachusetts' highest court denied the State's claims of privilege and ordered the DSS to release a large number of internal memoranda and similar d ocuments. As the Plaintiffs' attorneys had anticipated:

> The documents clearly show a scramble by aides to justify a predetermined policy rather than a well thought out policy arrived at with the help of experts[,] as had been claimed.[167]

The Settlement

As Donald Babets and David Jean approached the fifth anniversary of the removal of two foster children from their home, attorneys for both sides were attempting to negotiate an out-of-court resolution to the lawsuit. The documents released by the Commonwealth and official interviews with key DSS personnel painted a fairly clear picture: In the wake of the termination of the Babets and Jean placement, the DSS had attempted to exclude all lesbians and gay men from consideration as foster parents, regardless of their individual qualifications.

---

[166] Letter to members of Park Square Advocates/Gay & Lesbian Advocates and Defenders, the public interest law firm that is pursuing the foster care case, from Executive Director Kevin J. Cathcart, n.d.

[167] *Ibid.*

It was becoming clear, however, that a trial would be lengthy and expensive for all concerned. Moreover, attorneys for both sides had informally admitted that, if they lost in the trial court, they were prepared to file an immediate appeal. It was not inconceivable, then, that the litigation would drag on for another five years.

Finally, in April, 1990, agreement was reached over a set of proposed guidelines that were intended to replace the offending portion of CMR 7.101(1). The proposed regulations stated:

> The Department shall consider, consistent with the best interests of the child, the following placement resources:
>
> (g) placement in a child's own home
>
> (h) placement in family foster care with relatives, with consideration given to extended family members and persons chosen by the parent(s) for substitute care;
>
> (i) placement in family foster care with a married couple with parenting experience and with time available for parenting or with a person with parenting experience and with time available for parenting;
>
> (j) placement in family foster care with a married couple without parenting experience and with time available for parenting or with a person without parenting experience and with time available for parenting;
>
> (k) placement in community residential care.
>
> Every reasonable effort should be made first to place a child in accordance with (g) or (h) above.

Any placement made pursuant to (j) or (k) shall require the written approval of the Area Director.[168]

According to statements issued by the DSS and by attorneys for the Plaintiffs, the chief advantage of the proposed regulations was to return authority for placement decisions to individual caseworkers in the field. In addition, placements with single people with parenting experience no longer require the written approval of the Commissioner of Social Services. As Secretary of Human Services Philip Johnston noted, "We've been persuaded that the key factor should not be marital status but parenting experience."[169] Interestingly, prospective foster parents will continue to be required to state their sexual preference on applications forms.

The new regulations were subject to a 50-day period for public comment and officially went into effect in late May, 1990. Subsequently, a number of bills were filed in the Legislature in an attempt to reinstate the ban on lesbian and gay foster parents. As of this writing, it appeared that none of the bills had enough support to survive either the combined House and Senate process or the Dukakis veto that Plaintiffs' attorneys were confident would follow.[170]

---

[168] Agreement Reached in Foster Care Placement Lawsuit. (1990, April 4). Press release issued by the Executive Office of Human Services, Boston, Massachusetts.

[169] Longcope, K. (1990, April 5). Foster-care ban on gays is reversed. *Boston Globe*, 1, 8, p. 8.

[170] Tony Doniger, Co-counsel on the Babets/Jean case, personal communication, July 5, 1990.

CHAPTER SIX

The Impact of Law — The Legal Status of Lesbian and Gay Foster Parents

With regard to the regulation of foster care, each state is free to establish its own laws, guidelines, and policies. In practice, however, specific requirements for foster parents are almost never addressed at the level of the civil statutes of a particular state, and states' laws are, with few exceptions, neutral on the subject of lesbian and gay foster parenting. Almost all states, however, give a broad mandate to their social service systems to establish procedures for the evaluation, training, and review of foster parents, and there are great variations in practice across the United States.

As the Commonwealth of Massachusetts discovered when it surveyed states' rules governing foster care in 1985, policies regarding homosexual and other "non-traditional" placements are almost invariably unwritten. To make matters more complicated, social service departments in the majority of states are county-administered (so that both county *and* state systems are in place), which suggests that policies may be enacted or enforced inconsistently even within a particular state. In fact, it is not uncommon to find disparities in practice within a few miles of each other.

It should not be presumed, however, that social service agencies may exercise *carte blanche* in forming policies and instituting practices that affect the citizens of a state. In general, all policies that carry the force of law, as do those of an administrative agency such as a social service department, must comport with the broad guarantees of rights and liberties that are embodied in the U.S. Constitution and in the constitutions of the states. In other words, any policy enacted by an individual agency, city, county, or state is theoretically susceptible to analysis and attack on constitutional grounds.

In fact, however, legal issues relative to lesbian and gay foster parenting constitute an emerging area of law in which unresolved questions far outnumber reliable precedents. A complete review of all of the questions relevant to the legal status of lesbian and gay foster parents and potential foster parents, then, would be nearly impossible. In addition, the many experts who write, teach, litigate, and adjudicate in this area do not always agree with one another's analyses. There are simply too many unanswered questions of law, too many unpredictable variables, and too many state and regional variations in policy and practice to provide a definitive legal statement on lesbian and gay foster parenting. Instead, what follows is a discussion of some of the current legal theories and issues relevant to the subject.

First, there are no general, national policies or laws that have been interpreted to shed an unambiguous light on lesbian and gay foster parenting. Second, what individuals mean when they speak of "the law" encompasses a vast array of both processes and outcomes. "Law," that is, can include all of the following: federal and states' constitutions; the codified statutes of both the United States and of the individual states; county and municipal ordinances; executive orders (which may be issued by the President, as well as by governors, mayors, and other officials); legislation (promulgated either by Congress, a state's legislature, a county board, or a city council); case law (decisions in the federal and state courts at the trial and appellate levels); rules and regulations created by administrative or regulatory bodies at the national, state, county, and municipal level); and, to a more limited extent, conventions and practices that reflect public policy. These systems interact with and, occasionally, impinge upon one another, but they are all involved in the manufacture, interpretation, and enforcement of "law."

Finally, there are almost no legal precedents on a state-by-state basis that specifically address lesbian and gay foster parenting. In analyzing the status of lesbian and gay foster parents, then, it is necessary to examine (a) a state's "parenting policies" generally, as they are explicated, e.g., in custody or visitation cases involving lesbian or gay biological parents or in which a non-biologically related caretaker has petitioned for guardianship, adoption, or the establishment of a parental relationship with a child; (b) the presence or absence in the state or community of legal protections for lesbians and gay men, such as prohibitions against job or housing discrimination; and (c) other laws or policies that affect the legal status of lesbian and gay citizens (most notably, for example, criminal sodomy statutes).

Legal Issues

Generally, the legal issues relevant to lesbian and gay foster parenting fall into three broad categories.

"Per Se" Presumptions that Lesbians and Gay Men are Unfit to Serve as Parents

In the context of contested custody litigation, courts across the country have repeatedly addressed the issue of whether a gay or lesbian biological parent is "per se" unfit to hold custody of a child, to exercise unrestricted visitation, or to prevail in a guardianship or similar proceeding. The presumption that homosexual men and women are, by their very nature, unfit to act as parents is embodied in what are commonly called "per se" rules — rules than create an irrebuttable conclusion unrelated to any characteristic of the individual.

In some instances, courts have held that the fact of a parent's homosexuality, standing alone, is not sufficient to support the conclusion that the parent is unfit.[171] In other cases, judges have ruled that a parent's homosexuality automatically rendered the

---

[171] The Washington State Supreme Court in *Cabalquinto v. Cabalquinto* (1983) 100 Wash.2d 325, 669 P.2d 886, e.g., ruled that "homosexuality in and of itself is not a bar to custody or reasonable rights of visitation" (669 P.2d at 888); and the Virginia Supreme Court in *Doe v. Doe* (1981) 222 Va. 736, 284 S.E.2d 799 "decline[d] to hold that every lesbian mother or homosexual father is *per se* an unfit parent (284 S.E.2d at 806). The Virginia Supreme Court later reversed this ruling, however. See *Roe v. Roe* (1985) 228 Va. 722, 324 S.E.2d 691 (homosexuals unfit as a matter of law).

parent unsuitable, and have either refused to entertain any testimony to the contrary or have required no demonstration of actual harm to a child. In such venues, the unfitness of the gay or lesbian parent is treated as a judicial presumption that the opposing side is not permitted to challenge; homosexuality "per se" disqualifies the individual from prevailing in whatever conflict is at hand. As Hitchens points out in her review of successful and unsuccessful gay and lesbian custody cases across the country, "[n]o identifiable factors emerge to explain the discrepancy in outcomes."[172]

In states with a tradition of "per se" limitations on the rights of lesbian and gay biological parents, however, it is likely that lesbians and gay men may similarly be treated unfavorably in their attempts to become foster parents. Moreover, if a child is removed from an existing lesbian or gay foster home in such a jurisdiction — solely because of the parent's sexual orientation — the parent may have little standing to advance a "best interests of the child" argument.

Courts in many states, however, have ruled that a parent's sexual orientation may not be presumed to be a detrimental or disqualifying factor unless a direct and adverse impact on the child's welfare can actually be documented. These states include Alabama, Alaska, California, Colorado, Massachusetts, Maine, Michigan, New Jersey, New York, Oregon, Texas, Vermont, Virginia,[173] and Washington.[174] These victories for lesbian mothers and gay fathers show a willingness of some courts to rely on

---

[172] Hitchens, D. J. (1989). Family law. In Achtenberg, R. (Ed.), *Sexual orientation and the law* (pp. 1-1 to 1-107). NY: Clark-Boardman Co., Ltd., §103[1][a], p. 1-11.

[173] *Doe v. Doe, supra;* but see *Roe v. Roe* (1985) 228 Va. 722, 324 S.E.2d 691 (homosexuals unfit as a matter of law).

[174] Taken from summaries in the following: Hitchens, *supra;* Gutis, P. S. (1987, January 21). Homosexual parents winning some custody cases. *New York Times,* III:1; and O'Toole, M. T. (1989). Gay parenting: Myths and realities. *Pace Law Review, 9,* 129-164.

expert testimony and psychosocial research in the debunking of stereotypes and myths.[175]

Such cases, however — both gay parents' losses and their successes — may have limited application to foster parenting. On the one hand, the biological relationship between parents and their natural children is generally accorded special significance by the courts. Consequently, that relation enjoys a long tradition of legal protection, including constitutional guarantees that have not been held to be available to foster parents and children. In addition, standards for the removal of children from existing relationships, it may be argued, are different from the standards involved in the evaluation of prospective foster parents.

On the other hand, the presumption of lack of fitness of lesbians and gay men is the same in the case of natural or foster parents, and the courts' analysis of and response to that issue is analogous. The question, as always, is what legal standard a judge will apply to the facts of a particular case, even if she or he determines that a homosexual foster parent is not presumptively unfit.

In practice, lesbian and gay legal advocates have advanced the argument that the fairest policy is to permit the disqualification of a lesbian or gay foster parent only where there is a showing of actual or imminent harm to a child. Courts have called this proposition the "nexus standard" — referring, in this instance, to the necessity of demonstrating a link between a parent's sexual orientation and harm to a child. The absence of such a nexus is one of the legal challenges brought by the Plaintiffs in the Babets and Jean case.[176]

---

[175] Uhl, B. (1986-87) A new issue in foster parenting — gays. *Journal of Family Law,* 25 (3), 577-597, p. 587.

[176] Judges are theoretically required to apply the "nexus" criterian in states where case law supports it — e.g., California (*Nadler v. Superior Court* (1967) 255 Cal.App.2d 523, 63 Cal.Rptr. 352) and Massachusetts (*Bezio v. Patenaude* (1980) 381 Mass. 563, 410 N.E.2d 1207), although it is not always rigorously followed. A more protected position for lesbians and gay men, as well as for other "nontraditional" parents, could be secured if legislators addressed this issue and embodied the requirement of a demonstration of "present harm" in states' domestic relations laws. (*See* also O'Toole, *supra*.)

It is with regard to the nexus criterion that social science data and the testimony of experts in psychiatry, psychology, and child welfare may help to remove concerns about the alleged harm to children of living with homosexual parents. As discussed in Chapter Four, these concerns typically include fears that children will be molested, that they themselves will grow up to be gay or lesbian, and that children will be stigmatized or traumatized by living with gay parents. The first two of these can be dispensed with comparatively easily, since empirical data exist to rebut these claims.

The third issue, however — that of the harassment or ostracism of a child by neighbors or peers — is more complicated. Over and over judges have chosen to remove custody from or to limit visitation with a gay or lesbian biological parent because of a belief in the *potential* for children to be "stigmatized"by living in a gay household — even when they have received absolutely no evidence that a particular child has ever been ostracized, ridiculed, or harmed because of her or his family situation. Moreover, this is typically one of the most emotional concerns raised by opponents of lesbian and gay parenting. It represents a kind of fall-back position when appeals to stereotypes of child molestation or inappropriate gender roles have been nullified by rational evidence.

In defending Massachusetts' 1985 foster care policy, for instance, State Representative Marie Parente summed the issue up this way:

> I'm not arguing homosexuality. I'm arguing
> children. I know homosexuals. They're very warm
> and caring and loving. But being a foster child of
> gay parents is just too much for a child to take.
> How could you people wish this on a child? Why
> would you let a little child go out on the play-
> ground and face this kind of ridicule?[177]

---

[177] Pincus, E. (1988, July 31-August 6) Duke legislates foster care policy. *Gay Community News*, 16(4), 1.

There is no question that, in a homophobic society, to live openly as a lesbian or gay man is to be a potential target for abuse, rejection, discrimination, or worse. The same may be true of the children of gays and lesbians. To exclude lesbians and gay men from consideration as foster parents on the basis of such an argument, however, is to assert that society is correct in its prejudices and that it need never change. Such "blaming the victim" can never result in remedies for America's social ills.

The "stigma" imprecation, in any case, involves a tautological proposition. Not infrequently, for example, judges argue that the "mores of society" prevent them from leaving a child in the custody of its lesbian mother. In so doing, they fail to acknowledge that the courts are one of the institutions responsible for *creating* "the mores of society." The legal system does not merely reflect social prejudices, it perpetuates them and gives them effect.

More to the point, however, the assumption that children of lesbian or gay parents will always suffer from ridicule or rejection appears to be unfounded. In a *Harvard Law Review* survey of American custody and visitation cases involving gay or lesbian parents, the author found only one case in which evidence was offered that a child of a lesbian mother had actually been "stigmatized" (in this case, teased) by peers.[178]

Similarly, published social science studies suggest that children of lesbian or gay parents do not necessarily suffer from stigma. Hotvedt and Mandel, for example, found that sons of lesbian and heterosexual mothers showed no differences in peer relations and that daughters of lesbians actually had higher popularity ratings than daughters of heterosexual mothers.[179]

---

[178] Custody denials to parents in same-sex relationships: An equal protection analysis. (1989). *Harvard Law Review, 102*(3), pp. 617-636. (Citing *L. v. D.* (Missouri Court of Appeals 1982) 639 S.W.2d 240.)

[179] Hotvedt, M.E. & Mandel, J.B. (1982). Children of lesbian mothers. In W. Paul, J. D. Weinrich, J. C. Gonsiorek, & M. E. Hotvedt (Eds.), *Homosexuality: Social, psychological, and biological issues* (pp. 275-285). Beverly Hills, CA: Sage.

Polikoff commented on a follow-up study of the same group of children four years later:

> The [relevant research] suggests either that judicial concern about peer or community harassment is overstated, or that such harassment causes no special adjustment difficulties. For example, one study of fifty-six children of lesbian mothers and forty-eight children of heterosexual mothers found no significant differences between the children's reports of their popularity at school and in their neighborhood.
>
> [I]t is unwarranted to assume that the children of lesbian or gay parents will be subjected to teasing or ostracism more frequently than the children of heterosexual parents, or that harassment based on a parent's sexual orientation will be more troubling than harassment based on other reasons.[180]

Finally, the two heterosexual children of lesbian families interviewed by Ricketts and Achtenberg[181] reported that, although they worried that they *might* be harassed if the "secret" of their family was revealed, they had not, in reality, suffered such harassment. Both reported abandoning "social control" strategies such as secrecy by late adolescence, at a time when they felt more comfortable with themselves and more secure in their own sexual identities.[182]

---

[180] Polikoff, *supra*, pp. 568-569, citing Green, R., Mandel, J.B., Hotvedt, M.E., Gray, J. and Smith, L. (1986). Lesbian mothers and their children: A comparison with solo parent heterosexual mothers and their children. *Archives of Sexual Behavior, 15*(2), 167-184.

[181] Ricketts & Achtenberg, 1990, *supra*.

[182] Children's strategies for dealing with the fear that a parent's homosexuality will be discovered can include choosing not to bring friends into the home, referring to a parent's partner as an aunt or uncle, and so forth. *See, e.g.,* Bozett, F. W. (1988). Social control of identity by children of gay fathers. *Western Journal of Nursing Research, 10*(5), 550-565.

Significantly, the issue of ostracism and social pressure in the context of a "nontraditional" family has been subjected to legal analysis by the United States Supreme Court. In *Palmore v. Sidoti*, a divorced white father petitioned for a change of custody when his former wife married a black man.[183] The petitioner believed that his school-age daughter would be harmed by "environmental pressures" because her mother had chosen "a lifestyle unacceptable . . . to society."[184]

The Supreme Court rejected the father's argument and noted that:

> It would ignore reality to suggest that racial and ethnic prejudices do not exist or that all manifestations of those prejudices have been eliminated. There is a risk that a child living with a stepparent of a different race may be subject to a variety of pressures and stresses not present if the child were living with parents of the same racial or ethnic origin.
>
> . . .
>
> The Constitution cannot control such prejudices but neither can it tolerate them. Private biases may be outside the reach of the law, but the law cannot, directly or indirectly, give them effect.[185]

Although the Court's holding dealt specifically with prejudices that may pertain to interracial marriage, the Supreme Court of Alaska later relied on the language of the *Palmore* opinion in allowing a lesbian mother to retain custody of her son. The

---

[183] *Palmore v. Sidoti* (1984) 466 U.S. 429.

[184] *Ibid.*, p. 431.

[185] *Ibid.*, p. 433.

Court stated, "Simply put, it is impermissible to rely on any real or imagined social stigma attaching to Mother's status as a lesbian."[186]

An even stronger statement of this position was provided by a New Jersey court in a similar case involving the contested custody of two daughters. In ordering that custody would remain with the lesbian mother, the Court noted:

> [I]t may be that because the community is intolerant of [the mother's] differences[,] these girls may sometimes have to bear themselves with greater than ordinary fortitude. But this does not necessarily portend that their moral welfare or safety will be jeopardized. It is just as reasonable to expect that they will emerge better equipped to search out their own standards of right and wrong, better able to perceive that the majority is not always correct in its moral judgments, and better able to understand the importance of conforming their beliefs to the requirements of reason and tested knowledge, not the constraints of currently popular sentiment or prejudice.
>
> ...
>
> Instead of courage and the precept that people of integrity do not shrink from bigots, [removing custody from the mother] counsels the easy option of shirking difficult problems and following the course of expedience. Lastly, it diminishes [the children's] regard for the rule of human behavior, everywhere accepted, that we do not forsake those to whom we are indebted for love and nurture merely because they are held in low esteem by others.[187]

---

[186]   *S.N.E. v. R.L.B.* (Alaska 1985) 699 P.2d 875 at 879.

[187]   *M.P. v. S.P.* (1979) 169 N.J.Super. 425; 404 A.2d 1256 at 1263.

Constitutional Issues

A. Due Process

Briefly, "due process" refers to provisions of the Fourteenth Amendment and various state constitutions that protect citizens from arbitrary governmental intrusion in their lives. The Fourteenth Amendment requires that, before an important right can be violated by government, a citizen must be given the opportunity to be heard at a fair official proceeding.

As noted in Chapter One, courts routinely have held that the constitutional "liberty interest" that resides in the relationship between a biological parent and his or her children does not apply to foster parenting. Some commentators, therefore, have held that a state would be within its authority to remove a child from a lesbian or gay foster home, as was the case with Babets and Jean, without providing the foster parents with a procedural hearing.[188] Indeed, there is appellate case law on this point in the context of non-gay foster parents.[189]

A state's power to take such a step, however, is not necessarily unchecked. The foster care system is charged, as its first priority, with the protection of children and the defense of their best interests. The "best interests of the child" standard is, moreover, the gauge that judges generally are obligated to apply in assessing any disruption of a foster placement that might come before them in the forum of the courts. (At least theoretically, child welfare workers are bound by the same standard.)

If a child has lived in a lesbian or gay foster home and is bonded with that parent, termination of the placement — for no reason other than the foster parent's homosexuality — may

---

[188]   *See,* e.g., Uhl, *supra.*

[189]   Uhl, *supra,* reviews these cases, pp. 589-591.

constitute a clear violation of the child's "best interests." A similar issue may arise if a foster child living in a gay or lesbian home becomes available for adoption, after customary termination and permanency-planning proceedings, but the agency refuses to consider the gay or lesbian foster parent as a potential adoptive parent. Arguably, in such a situation, the child could have a cause of action, through a guardian ad litem, for the agency's failure to promote her or his best interests.

Perhaps more sophisticated and less well grounded in legal precedent might be a class-action suit on behalf of the class of foster children denied private-home placements because of a state's or county's refusal to consider possible lesbian and gay homes. There is, of course, more than sufficient evidence to support the proposition that multiple or disrupted placements are harmful to foster children, and that most children fare better in private homes than in group or institutional settings.

On the other hand, a growing body of case law and legal theory suggests that some courts may be willing to expand concepts of family to give legal standing to socially and emotionally related others who have bonded with children and are important in their lives. These cases do not pertain directly to foster parenting, but they do touch on constitutional issues of concern to gay and lesbian foster parents. Theoretically, at least, if a non-biologically related individual is permitted standing to bring a legal proceeding (e.g., a petition to establish "de facto" parent status or a request for visitation), the court has acknowledged the individual's constitutionally protected interest in preserving the family relationship that he or she has developed with a child.

That is, in fact, one of the determinations that a Florida appellate court made in awarding custody of an eight-year-old girl (Kristen) to the lesbian partner (Neenie) of the girl's deceased biological mother. In so doing, the court simultaneously vacated the adoption of Kristen by her grandparents and noted that Kristen's welfare would best be served by returning her to the custody of her "de facto" parent, Neenie, with whom she had lived all her life.[190]

The court cited similar decisions in Colorado[191] and California,[192] and noted a recently enacted Oregon statute that permits anyone "who has established emotional ties creating a parent-child relationship to petition for custody or visitation."[193] Laws similar to the Oregon statute are based on the theory of "in loco parentis" and seek to recognize relationships in which an adult (or adults) has stood "in the place of a parent" with respect to a particular child.

In a California case related to *In re Pearlman*, an appeals court considered the situation of a four-year-old girl, Martha, whose mother had committed suicide.[194] Martha's grandmother was appointed legal guardian, but Kenneth T., a friend of the family, petitioned for visitation. Kenneth argued that he had contributed to Martha's support for more than three years, had developed a loving relationship with her, and considered himself her "psychological father." Martha's grandmother opposed the proceeding on the ground that Kenneth was a "stranger," but the court recognized Kenneth's right, as an interested but legally or biologically unrelated person, to seek visitation with the minor child.

Although these cases have potential precedential value to foster parents, they could, obviously, be applied only in situations in which a lesbian or gay parent had lived with and cared for a

---

[190] *In re Pearlman*, 15 Family Law Reporter (BNA) 1355 (Florida Circuit Court, Broward County, March 31, 1989).

[191] *In re Hatzopoulos*, 4 Family Law Reporter (BNA) 2075 (Denver County Juvenile Court, November 15, 1977).

[192] *In re the Matter of Brian Todd Batey*, San Diego Superior Court, Case Number 134752. *See* Mother loses: Lover gets custody of gay man's son. (1987, November 6). *San Francisco Chronicle*.

[193] *In re Pearlman, supra*. *See* also Polikoff, *supra*, for an in-depth discussion of the Oregon statute and related parenthood strategies.

[194] *Guardianship of Martha M.* (1988), 88 California Daily Opinion Service 6814.

foster child and, thus, had established the kind of relationship contemplated in the Oregon statute and in the dicta of the various opinions. Still, taken as a whole, they reflect a growing willingness to deal with non-traditional family constellations and with the "alternative" realities of many children's lives.

A more traditional due process argument, however, does involve the right of gay men and lesbians to be evaluated fairly as prospective foster parents, and to stand on equal footing with all other applicants, regardless of their sexual orientation. As Hitchens notes:

> Strict compliance [with due process requirements] means, among other things, that the use of conclusive presumptions, legislative or judicial, is impermissible.[195]

The application of "per se" rules to the lesbian or gay prospective foster parent would thus violate due process requirements because no lesbian or gay individual could participate fairly in the procedure by which foster parents are licensed. This automatic exclusion of lesbian and gay applicants was another of the plaintiffs' complaints in the Boston foster care case.[196]

---

[195] Hitchens, *supra*, pp. 1-64 - 1-65.

[196] It is fair to note that the Massachusetts DSS always maintained that its priority system did not "exclude" gay or lesbian foster parents. Indeed, language to that effect does not appear in the regulation. The fact that no placements were made with known lesbian or gay foster parents after the promulgation of CMR 7.101 in 1985, however, indicates that such a process of elimination was practiced, if not explicitly mandated in the regulation. The irony of the Commonwealth's position is reflected in the fact that the individual plaintiffs in the lawsuit were routinely reviewed and re-approved as foster parents each year, although they were never considered for a subsequent placement. Recall, too, that when the policy was first presented, Secretary of Human Services Philip Johnston pronounced future lesbian and gay foster placements "highly unlikely" (Cooper, May 25, 1985, *supra*, p. 24).

B. Equal Protection

Also embodied in the Fourteenth Amendment to the U.S. Constitution is a guarantee that, when the state makes a distinction between two classes of people for the purpose of granting or denying some right or privilege, there will be a rational basis for the distinction. Hitchens observes:

> If the right is deemed to be "fundamental" or the classification deemed "suspect," then the state bears a heavy burden of showing that the distinction is "necessary to promote a compelling government interest" (citations omitted).[197]

In the Boston foster care case one of the plaintiffs' constitutional challenges involved the state's practice of dividing prospective foster parents into categories of greater or lesser desirability based on their sexual orientation.

Since 1985, that is, all Massachusetts foster parenting applicants have been required to indicate their sexual preference on application forms. If an applicant identifies her- or himself as a lesbian or gay man (or declines to answer the question), the application is treated differently from any other. The prospective foster parent automatically falls into a category that requires the Department of Social Services' highest level of review. Moreover, such individuals are extremely unlikely ever to receive a child.

This practice constitutes "making a distinction" between groups of people for "the purpose of granting or denying some right or privilege" (even if it is only the right to be considered or the privilege of being evaluated). Theoretically, then, the state should be required to show that the differential treatment is necessary to achieve a "compelling" purpose of government — which, in this case, is the protection of children and the service of their needs.

---

[197]   Hitchens, *supra*, pp. 1-65 - 1-66.

In Uhl's summary,

> Since the objective of the [Massachusetts] policy is
> to provide a warm, stable, nurturing home for a
> child, the question to be answered becomes: are
> homosexual couples, because of their sexual
> preference ... any less capable of providing a
> warm, stable, nurturing home and [are they] not
> similarly situated to a heterosexual, married couple
> .... [T]he recent case law dealing with this matter
> supports the view that this presumption of a
> homosexual's lack of fitness to be a parent should
> not be made in the courtroom, by statute or implic-
> itly by policies ... promulgated by a state agency.
> Given this view, it can be concluded that a hetero-
> sexual couple and a homosexual couple may be
> similarly situated with respect to their child-rearing
> abilities, unless evidence to the contrary is of-
> fered.[198]

The level of judicial scrutiny to which such a policy must be
subjected, however, and the weight of the burden any state must
bear in justifying its policy, have been the subject of considerable
differences of legal opinion. In general, lesbians and gay men
have not been held to be a "suspect class" for purposes of equal
protection analysis, a distinction that would require laws or
regulations involving sexual preference-based distinctions to be
"strictly" scrutinized by a reviewing court. ("Strict scrutiny" is
the third, highest level of equal protection analysis.) Nor, as has
already been noted, has foster parenting *per se* been considered a
right.

The U.S. Supreme Court, in particular, has not ruled on the
question of whether to impose this higher level of scrutiny on
laws and policies that affect homosexual men and women, although some lower courts have held that lesbians and gay men
are entitled to "suspect" class status for purposes of equal

---

[198]   Uhl, *supra*, p. 529.

protection review.[199] In the event "strict scrutiny" were to be applied in an actual lawsuit, Hitchens notes,

> [T]he state would have little difficulty in establishing a compelling interest in protecting the welfare of ... children, [although] the required showing that the distinction drawn be "necessary" to accomplish that objective cannot be made since no nexus has ever been proven between the sexual orientation of a parent and the children's welfare .... The court may not ... draw distinctions that are based on "mere negative attitudes or fear, unsubstantiated by factors which are properly cognizable" (citations omitted).[200]

Given the large and growing body of social science information on lesbian and gay parenting, the support of mental health and child welfare experts (such as the 41 groups who spoke out against the Massachusetts policy), and the professional guidelines enacted by the American Psychiatric Association, the American Psychological Association, and the National Association of Social Workers (see Appendix C), there would indeed seem to be little basis upon which to argue that the rejection of lesbian and gay foster parenting applicants bears a rational relationship to promoting the welfare of children.

Anti-Sodomy Laws

Prior to 1961, all states and the District of Columbia had laws on their books against sodomy. As of this writing, 28 states have rescinded these laws, while 22 states and the District of Columbia retain them. Penalties range from maximum jail sentences of

---

[199] *See*, e.g., Hitchens, *supra*, pp. 1-66 - 1-67, citing *Watkins v. U.S. Army* (1988) 837 F.2d 1428 (9th Cir.), *reh'g granted*, 847 F.2d 1329 (9th Cir.); and *High Tech Gays v. Defense Industry Security Clearance Office* (N.D. Cal. 1987) 668 F.Supp. 1361.

[200] *Ibid.*

20 days (e.g., in Georgia) to small fines elsewhere. States with sodomy laws applying both to homosexuals and heterosexuals include Alabama, Arizona, Florida, Georgia,[201] Idaho, Louisiana, Maryland, Massachusetts, Minnesota, Mississippi, Montana, North Carolina, Oklahoma, Rhode Island, South Carolina, Utah, Virginia, and the District of Columbia. Laws applicable to homosexual sodomy only exist in Arkansas, Kansas, Missouri, Nevada, and Tennessee.

In 1986, the United States Supreme Court ruled in *Bowers v. Hardwick*,[202] a Georgia case involving a gay man arrested, in his own bedroom, for engaging in oral sex with another man. The *Hardwick* opinion has been subjected to extensive analysis in the years since, but its most basic effect is to permit states to continue to define sodomy and to enact laws against it without fear of "a constitutional challenge based on federal constitutional privacy doctrines."[203]

In other words, there is no constitutionally protected right to sexual privacy, and states are free to set limits as their legislators see fit. Although Georgia's anti-sodomy law was not limited to same-sex contact and prohibited marital heterosexual sodomy as well, the Supreme Court Justices focused almost exclusively on homosexual sodomy in their opinion. Gay rights activists were dismayed by the ruling, fearing that it would encourage anti-homosexual legislation.

Since *Hardwick*, in fact, several states, including Kentucky, have amended their anti-sodomy laws to decriminalize heterosexual sodomy and to encompass only same-sex sexual activity. A Georgia appellate court, in addition, recently declared that state's anti-sodomy statute unconstitutional as to heterosex-

---

[201] But *see* discussion of *Mosley v. Esposito, infra.*

[202] 478 U.S. 186; 106. S.Ct. 2841.

[203] Rivera, R. R. (1987). Legal issues in gay and lesbian parenting. In F. W. Bozett (Ed.), *Gay and lesbian parents* (pp. 199-227). New York: Praeger Press, p. 200.

ual married couples only. Citing *Hardwick* as precedent for specific prohibitions against homosexual sodomy, the Court wrote "Government has no business with a married couple's private consensual practices."[204]

Sodomy laws have, for years, been used to justify restrictions on visitation with or removal of custody from a lesbian or gay biological parent. Commonly, anti-sodomy statutes are specifically cited in adverse opinions as, for example, in *Roe v. Roe*,[205] a Virginia Supreme Court case in which the Justices removed the custody of a child from her gay father and severely restricted his visitation. There, the Court repeatedly cited the father's "illicit" and "unlawful" behavior (which, the Court noted, was likely to continue since the father lived with his male lover).

As Ricketts and Achtenberg point out:

> Although [anti-sodomy] laws are rarely enforced, their existence has been a significant negative influence upon judicial decision-making in the custody and visitation arena, and there is every reason to suspect a corollary effect with respect to adoption and foster parenting.[206]

The authors go on to describe an illustration of that effect taken from the proceedings of the Pima County, Arizona juvenile court.[207] In that instance, an openly bisexual applicant for pre-adoption certification was thoroughly investigated by the state DSS and was pronounced qualified. During the hearing upon the application, however, and prompted by his apparent belief in the threat to children that the applicant posed, the trial judge asked the applicant whether he would molest a child placed in his custody or would attempt to "convert" a child to homosexuality.

---

[204] *Mosley v. Esposito*, No. 89-6897-1 (Superior Court, DeKalb County).

[205] *Roe v. Roe, supra.*

[206] Ricketts & Achtenberg, 1987, *supra*, p. 94.

[207] *Ibid.*, citing *In re Pima County Juvenile Action*, 12 Family Law Reporter (BNA) 1557 (Arizona Court of Appeals, 1986).

Ultimately, the judge denied the application on the ground that "[p]etitioner is a bisexual individual who has had, and may in future have, sexual relationships with members of both sexes."

In upholding the decision, the Arizona Appellate Court reasoned that while the applicant's bisexuality, standing alone, would be an insufficient basis on which to deny him certification, his homosexual conduct, proscribed by Arizona anti-sodomy laws, was. The court stated:

> It would be anomalous for the state on one hand to declare homosexual conduct unlawful and on the other hand [to] create a parent after that proscribed model, in effect approving that standard, inimical to the natural family, as head of a state-created family.

In states with *both* anti-sodomy laws and a practice of applying "per se" presumptions of unfitness to homosexual parents, it may be unrealistic to expect that lesbian and gay foster parents (or applicants) will be protected by the courts or legislature.

The New Hampshire Case

In the wake of the Boston Foster care case, a number of jurisdictions considered similar bans or limitations on lesbian and gay foster parents. As of this writing, however, only the State of New Hampshire had gone so far as to enact such a prohibition. The New Hampshire case is interesting because the Legislature anticipated the very constitutional and sodomy-related issues that have been discussed here.

After the original legislation was introduced in March, 1987, and while it was still pending in the House of Representatives, the House Judiciary Committee asked the New Hampshire Supreme Court to render its advisory opinion on the constitutionality of the proposed new law (House Bill 70).

In their official Opinion, returned two months later, four of the Justices resolved that no violations of state or federal constitutional rights of due process, equal protection, privacy, or assembly would occur if the proposed ban on lesbian and gay foster and adoptive parents were to be enacted.

Their reasoning took two major paths. First, they accepted the Legislature's suggestion that homosexual parents would negatively influence foster or adoptive children. They concluded that

> the exclusion of homosexuals from [adoption and
> foster parenting] bears a rational relationship to the
> government's legitimate objective of providing ...
> children with appropriate parental role models ....
> The classification created here embodies a predic-
> tion of a risk not immediately disprovable by
> contrary evidence ... and it addresses a risk of
> harm that would not be readily reversible in those
> cases in which it could be expected to occur.[208]

As a result, they wrote, any attack on due process or equal protection grounds would fail. In a passionate dissent accompanying the majority opinion, Justice William F. Batchelder argued these same points:

> The bill presumes that every homosexual is unfit to
> be an adoptive parent or to provide foster care ....
> Financial stability is irrelevant; the strength to
> discipline a child firmly yet patiently is irrelevant;
> and the courage and love to be generous and loyal,
> the intelligence to provide proper education, and
> similar attributes are all irrelevant. Yet the legisla-
> ture has no rational basis for concluding that
> homosexuals will be deficient in these characteris-
> tics ....
>
> The legislature received no meaningful evidence to
> show that homosexual parents endanger their
> children's development of sexual preference,
> gender role identity, or general physical and psy-
> chological health any more than heterosexual
> parents. The legislature received no such evidence
> because apparently the overwhelming weight of

---

[208] Opinion of the Justices. New Hampshire House of Representatives. *7 May 87 House Record*, 2505 - 2515, p. 2511.

professional study on the subject concludes that no
difference in psychological and psychosexual
development can be discerned between children
raised by heterosexual parents and children raised
by homosexual parents.[209]

The majority Justices, however, in the second prong of their
argument, went on to dispense with the remaining two constitutional considerations. They wrote:

[T]here is no privacy-grounded right to engage in
consensual homosexual sodomy; [therefore] there
is no corresponding right to freedom of association
for such a purpose.[210]

At first glance, it may seem illogical that the question of
sodomy even arises in this context. It was here, however, that the
direct impact of anti-sodomy laws on homosexual foster parenting
was felt. In drafting House Bill 70, the authors specifically stated
that their intention had been to follow "public policy" as set out in
Bowers v. Hardwick.[211] The Justices merely conformed to the
Legislature's lead in expanding the *Hardwick* analysis.

In specific, the New Hampshire legislature borrowed the
language of *Hardwick* to identify the group of people that it intended to prohibit from adopting or providing foster care. In
excluding "homosexuals" from consideration as adoptive or foster
parents, the relevant statute (adopted in July, 1987) reads:

"Homosexual" means any person who knowingly
and voluntarily performs or submits to any sexual

---

[209]   *Ibid.*, p. 2513.

[210]   *Ibid.*, p. 2512.

[211]   *See* annotation following New Hampshire Rev. Stat. Ann., Public Safety and
Welfare Code, Chap. 170-B:4, "Legislative intent."

act involving the sex organs of one person and the mouth or anus of another person of the same gender.[212]

This is essentially the language of the *Hardwick* opinion, which was itself taken from the Georgia anti-sodomy statute. Ironically, New Hampshire repealed its own anti-sodomy laws some years ago, and the behavior that is described in Chapter 170-B:2(XV) is no longer criminal in the state.[213] As Justice Batchelder pointed out in his dissent from the majority Opinion, in addition, adultery remains criminal in New Hampshire; yet there was no suggestion in the proposed bill that prospective heterosexual foster or adoptive parents be required to state whether or not they had committed adultery.

Clearly, however, the Justices were not interested in criminality per se, but rather in the definition of the class of persons who were to be excluded from adopting or from providing foster care. In fact, an earlier draft of the legislation was returned to the Judiciary Committee by the Justices with a request that the authors define the term "homosexual." The first report of House Bill 70 contained no *Hardwick*-related language.

---

[212] *See* New Hampshire Rev. Stat. Ann., Public Safety and Welfare Code, Chap. 170-B:2(XV). Foster parenting certification forms include the question, "Are you, or is any adult in your household, a homosexual within the statutory definition?".

[213] In April, 1990, the Civil Liberties Union of New Hampshire launched a limited challenge to the state's ban on lesbian and gay foster parents. The lawsuit involves two plaintiffs, a minister and his wife, who had sought licensure as emergency foster care providers. Both refused to answer the sexual orientation question on the grounds of privacy. As expected, they were not licensed. By definition, however, "emergency" foster shelter in New Hampshire is limited to 30 days, and the plaintiffs argue that "inappropriate role modeling" could not occur in so short a time. They intend to show that the exclusion of homosexuals (or of people who decline to reveal their sexual orientation) from consideration as emergency foster parents is invalid if based on the "role-modeling" theory embedded in the statute. Plaintiffs hope that this preliminary challenge will ultimately undermine the prohibition entirely.

Yale legal scholar Janet Halley, however, points out that
characterizing sodomy as the "behavior that defines the class" (of
lesbians and gay men) is becoming an increasingly common
practice in the law, particularly in the context of equal protection
arguments.[214]

To the extent that anti-sodomy laws continue to be invoked to
create a class of people who are either already criminals (by virtue
of existing laws) or are potentially criminals (since, after *Hardwick*,
any "free" state can re-enact such laws), anti-sodomy statutes
cannot help but have an adverse impact on lesbians and gay men
in all areas of public interface.[215]

Halley makes the fascinating and instructive observation,
however, that the practices outlined in anti-sodomy statutes by no
means describe the sexual behavior of every individual who
nevertheless identifies as lesbian or gay. Sociologists Blumstein
and Schwartz, for example, reported in their study of "American
couples" that 23 percent of lesbians did not engage in oral sex.[216]
Further, Halley argues,

> [T]he many gay men who have abandoned fellatio
> and anal intercourse to protect themselves and
> their lovers from AIDS, self-identified gay men and
> lesbians who remain celibate — [according to
> *Hardwick*-based criteria] none of these groups
> belong to the class "homosexual."[217]

---

[214]   Halley, J. E. (1989). The politics of the closet: Towards equal protection for
        gay, lesbian, and bisexual identity. *UCLA Law Review, 36*, 915-976; *see*, in
        particular, pp. 918-920 & pp. 948 et seq.

[215]   In Dallas, Texas, for example, a lesbian was recently denied employment as
        a police officer because of Texas's anti-sodomy law. *See* Lambda sues Texas
        on sodomy-related discrimination. (1990, June). *Lesbian/Gay Law Notes*, p.
        40.

[216]   Blumstein, P. & Schwartz, P. (1983). *American couples.* NY: William Morrow.

[217]   Halley, *supra*, p. 949.

Put another way, there is a potentially significant number of self-proclaimed lesbians and gay men in New Hampshire who are not homosexual, according to the legal definition, and who are thus arguably entitled to provide foster care or to become adoptive parents.

That theoretical distinction aside, what Halley describes (and what is embodied in the New Hampshire statute) is a failure to distinguish between "status" and "conduct." A useful constitutional argument would focus on the differential treatment experienced by persons who are assigned to the status of "homosexual" — either voluntarily or because someone in authority has applied that label to them.

Once the label is assigned, of course, the characteristics assumed to be true of the class are assumed to be true of the individual as well. The legal issue then becomes to identify which elements of society have the ability to assign these characteristics and to make such assumptions. In this way, what emerges is an analysis of power relations, an exploration of the ways in which governments are able to confer or withhold benefits based on distinctions government has made and predicated on sets of beliefs that government is in a position to enforce.

From a legal perspective, much work remains to be done in analyzing the distinctions themselves, the impartiality of the structures that hold them in place, and the availability of redress to citizens whose individuality may have been diminished in the process.

CHAPTER SEVEN

Putting the Issues in Context — Final Considerations and Additional Resources

As we enter the 1990s, Americans are embroiled in a profound reconsideration of their values and of the meaning of American life. That process is proving to be both painful and passionate. Almost without warning, we find ourselves re-fighting basic battles over obscenity, censorship in the arts, and free speech. We watch as deep-seated fears over America's drug crisis and the AIDS epidemic lead lawmakers to embrace the suspension of privacy rights, freedom from unwarranted search and seizure, the privilege against self-incrimination, and other traditional constitutional liberties. And we cannot help but be cynical when our leaders include those who view flag-burning as a greater menace to national integrity than growing poverty and homelessness.

At the same time, we are witnessing the resurgence of violent racism on college campuses and in our neighborhoods; a retrench- ment of the civil rights victories of the 60s and 70s; a new squeamishness regarding women's reproductive rights; a re- characterization of affirmative action strategies as "entitlement programs" for less qualified or less ambitious individuals; and the accusation that the social justice agenda of the past 35 years has become little more than a forum for the tyranny of special-interest groups.

Even within the more private realm of the family, there is far-reaching change — change that encompasses significant demographic shifts as well new consciousness and language. Phrases such as "broken home," "living in sin," and "unwed mother," for example, represent concepts rarely used to describe modern familial and interpersonal relationships, although they belong to the very recent past. Divorce no longer carries with it the social stigma of only a generation ago; and "mixed" marriages — couples of different races or religions — have ceased to pose the impossible conundrum they once did for our culture.

The purpose and meaning of our intimate relationships, moreover, have begun to reflect a host of new expectations and considerations — even as our reasons for choosing to bear and raise children are marked by changes of their own.

Finally, we are beginning to recognize that idealistic visions of family life must stand alongside increasingly candid discussions of the sexual abuse, physical violence, substance addiction, and emotional impoverishment that have also been a hidden, but undeniable presence in the American family. These powerful and varied forces, together with the impact of so much new information and awareness, have profoundly shaken American lives.

When it comes to parenting, children, and family life, however, nearly all of us continue to hold strong, deeply personal views. Place discussion of these topics in the context of conflicting national political trends, and combine it with controversial issues such as homosexuality and the needs of America's foster children, and it becomes clear why lesbian and gay foster parenting provokes such heated debate.

For all sides, the stakes are high. For millions of lesbians and gay men, the issues are nothing less than justice and the recognition of their full humanity. For opponents of gay and lesbian rights, acceptance of homosexuality seems to shake the very foundations of morality and family life.

For child welfare and helping professionals, there are other considerations as well. Most of our country's foster care systems are critically overburdened, and there is no shortage anywhere of children in desperate need. It is no small responsibility to be charged with the shelter and protection of such children.

How is it possible then, to acknowledge the strong feelings Americans have about homosexuality, about caring for children, and about the necessity of promoting fair government practices — and at the same time to develop a policy for dealing with lesbian and gay foster parents that is just and free from unwarranted discrimination? Indeed, such conflicts have constituted a basic dilemma of American democracy for hundreds of years — and they continue to do so today.

We know, for example, that many Americans still believe they should not have to live or work alongside Blacks; that Jews and other non-"Aryans" are bringing about the downfall of American society; that people are poor due solely to laziness and weakness of character; that women have overstepped tolerable limits in challenging male authority; and that Asians — whether as investors or immigrants — are responsible for the economic crises facing America's working class.

We may not applaud these beliefs, but we know they exist. Indeed, we are often confronted with their tragic consequences — the Vincent Chin murder,[218] for example, the incidents at Howard Beach, the desecrations of synagogues and Jewish cemeteries across America, and the startling fact that more American women are killed by their husbands each year than die in automobile accidents.[219]

Yet even while we acknowledge that many Americans hold beliefs such as those described above, we do not feel compelled to make these sentiments the basis of national policies and state laws. Most of our existing laws, that is, intentionally fail to accommodate the entire spectrum of philosophical and personal differences that divide us. Instead, we have determined somehow to make our way to higher ground, and to formulate law and policy that reflect a broader concept of social justice and the public good.

The road to that high ground has sometimes been rocky. At times, we have struggled to locate an ethical position amid

---

[218] Professor Mari J. Matsuda writes, "Vincent Chin was a 27-year-old Chinese-American beaten to death by baseball-bat-wielding thugs in Detroit. The assailants yelled, 'It's because of you fucking J[ap]s that we're out of work.'" *In* Public responses to racist speech: Considering the victim's story. (1989, August). *Michigan Law Review, 87*, 2320-2381, p. 2330, fn.55.

[219] Esta Soler, Executive Director, Family Violence Project (San Francisco, California). Speech at "New Arguments Against the Death Penalty," ACLU of Northern California Annual Conference, Berkeley, California, July 8, 1990.

generations and even centuries of "common knowledge," scientific "fact," simple prejudice, and a hearty reluctance to rock the boat. With regard to women, people of color, and many other groups, as the examples suggest, those struggles are not yet complete.

Lesbians and gay men, too, have experienced a long tradition of discrimination in America — the denial of access to jobs, housing, and other basic rights; the devaluation of their intimate relationships; the debilitating effects of negative stereotypes; the constant threat of physical violence. Indeed, although lesbians and gay men form one of the largest minority groups in the United States, many (perhaps most) Americans could not name a close friend or relative whom they knew to be gay or lesbian.

For some, the relative invisibility of lesbians and gay men and the lack of access to accurate information about their lives makes it difficult to know how or why an anti-homosexual position should be changed. At the same time, the systematic and intentional nature of a tradition of persecution, enforced invisibility, and disenfranchisement of lesbians and gay men continues to be expressed in our nation's laws, court decisions, educational policies, and the like.

Equally longstanding, however, is the fight against such forms of oppression. Throughout our history, periods of retrenchment and intolerance have been balanced by periods of healing and of greater concern for social equity. Indeed, over the last two decades, scores of human service organizations, human rights advocates, legal and professional assemblies, and even churches have encouraged society to re-examine its attitudes toward and treatment of gay men and lesbians. The lesbian and gay movement, that is, has taken its place in America's long history of organized opposition to racism, sexism, classism, and other oppressive systems.

Today, America continues to confront not only its familiar fears and prejudices regarding color, class, and gender, but new ones related to sexual orientation and to AIDS. These concerns, too, are part of America's historical commitment to social justice. In weighing the many issues raised by lesbian and gay foster parenting, that history provides an essential perspective.

Is Sexual Orientation Irrelevant?

Given the differential treatment experienced by gay men and lesbians in America today, it would be difficult to argue that a foster parent's homosexuality had no bearing whatsoever on a placement decision. But what weight should sexual orientation be given among the host of other factors that may also affect the life of a foster child — including the prospective parent's race, economic status, gender, education, parenting experience, relationship status, and physical and psychological health?

Indeed, if sexual orientation is judged to be a critical factor, it is important to consider how the significance of sexual orientation will be assessedfor all prospective foster parents — and not just those known to be lesbian or gay. Are there situations, for example, in which a foster parent's *heterosexuality* makes him or her a less ideal placement? If a child has been repeatedly abused by men in a heterosexual home, for example, might there be particular benefits to a foster placement with a lesbian couple?

With regard to the significance of foster parents' sexual orientation, however, there is another matter to consider. Virtually all children and adolescents in foster care — including the victims of physical and sexual abuse; the neglected, discarded, and unloved ones; the babies born with drug addictions and AIDS — all begin life in heterosexual homes. Their heterosexual parents have rejected them, are incapable of giving them love or nurturing, or can no longer provide for their material needs.

Given the fact that heterosexual parents have demonstrated, in case after case, their capacity to harm children in their care, why do lesbians and gay men so often confront the assumption that they are unfit to act as parents? Indeed, if heterosexuality were as closely associated with capable, committed parenting as it is presumed to be, would we need a foster care system at all?

These points are not raised for the sake of being controversial, but in the hope of exposing the framework within which questions are asked about the fitness of lesbian and gay foster parents and about the impact of sexual orientation on foster children. In the long view, it is less important whether such an examination leads to approval of gay and lesbian foster parents. What does matter, however, is that child welfare professionals consider what it really means to protect the best interests of children.

Gay and Lesbian Youth in Foster Care

Given the attention that is often focused on the sexual orientation of prospective foster parents, it is ironic that the sexual orientation of adolescents and teenagers in foster care is all but ignored. For one large group of foster children, however — gay, lesbian, bisexual, "questioning," and other sexual minority   youth — sexual orientation issues are of utmost concern. What is more, these individuals form a significant proportion of the population requiring foster care. Ricketts and Achtenberg[220] cite informal estimates that from 30-70 percent of the juvenile prostitute, street, and runaway population are lesbian or gay youth.

These young people may enter the child-welfare system through the juvenile courts, through child-protective services, or through runaway, street-outreach, or suicide-prevention programs.[221] Often these are children who have grown up harboring a guilty secret — a secret hidden even from the family members upon whom they depend most. When they reveal their homosexuality, they are frequently abused physically or emotionally and driven from their homes. Ricketts and Achtenberg, for example, report an interview with "Casey," a gay teenager ordered out of his home at gunpoint by his mother.[222]

---

[220]   Ricketts & Achtenberg, 1990, *supra*, p. 94.

[221]   Social worker Paul Gibson reports that gay youths are 2-3 times more likely to attempt suicide than other young people, and that suicide is the leading cause of death among sexual minority youth. *See* Gay male and lesbian youth suicide. (1989, January). In M. R. Feinleib (Ed.), *Report of the Secretary's Task Force on Youth Suicide — Volume 3: Prevention and Interventions in Youth Suicide* (pp. 3-110 - 3-142). U.S. Department of Health and Human Services. Alcohol, Drug Abuse and Mental Health Administration. Washington, D.C.: Government Printing Office.

[222]   Ricketts & Achtenberg, *supra*, pp. 95-96.

If lesbian, gay, or bisexual youth find their way into the adolescent social service delivery system — and into foster care in particular — it is not uncommon for them to experience a series of unsuccessful placements with families or in group homes in which their homosexual feelings and behavior are discouraged, ridiculed, ignored, or punished. On this point, Ricketts and Achtenberg quote Steve Ashkinazy, a social worker at New York City's Hetrick-Martin Institute for the Protection of Lesbian and Gay Youth. Regarding the in-service training programs that his organization offers to personnel in adolescent shelters and group homes, Ashkinazy noted:

> We've had many situations where agency staff
> have blatantly told us that they were not interested
> in changing their attitudes. They didn't want us to
> tell them that homosexuality was OK, because they
> knew it was not. When you have staff who really
> believe it isn't OK to be gay, there's no real possi-
> bility that a gay person, especially an adolescent,
> could stay there without developing negative
> feelings about him- or herself. Some group homes
> are better than others, but there are no group
> homes in New York that are fully comfortable for a
> gay kid. In some, it would not be realistic to think
> a gay kid could survive there at all.[223]

In several cities, however, a growing number of public and private agencies are beginning to view lesbian and gay homes as appropriate placements for homosexually-identified and other sexual minority youth. The city of Los Angeles's Triangle Project, for example, has been remarkably successful in recruiting and training gay and lesbian parents for children (both gay and straight) who need foster homes.

---

[223] *Ibid.*, p. 95. *See also* the interview with "Rhonda," a 16-year-old lesbian who described her experiences in a group foster home: "They watched every-thing I did. They made me sign an agreement not to touch any other girl in the home. They totally blew the subject out of proportion." *Id.*, pp. 96-97.

Since its inception, the Triangle Project has worked jointly with the Los Angeles County Department of Social Services, whose personnel attend Triangle recruitment meetings in order to facilitate the process of becoming foster parents. Triangle's meetings often include talks by current lesbian or gay foster parents or by lesbian or gay youth who have lived in foster care. One such individual is "Tim."

Twenty-one at the time he was interviewed, Tim was placed in a gay foster home several years before the inception of the Triangle program. His foster father, "Tony," was a high school English teacher who had cared for more than 25 foster children, gay and straight. Like Tim, Tony was also gay, although he felt he could not be open about it until Tim was nearly 18.

A Gay Teenager in Foster Care: Tim

When Tim was 6 years old, his mother made what was at least her 12th suicide attempt. Tim wasn't sure of the number, although he does remember that it took place on Christmas Eve. At that point, the county's Child Protective Service finally decided to intervene. They broke up the family of seven brothers and sent them to four different foster homes.

As a sixteen-year-old, and after nearly eleven years in various foster care settings, Tim was placed with Tony. Today, Tim describes himself as "the only survivor of my biological family." After turning 18, Tim continued to live with Tony and Tony's other foster children.

Before I moved in with Tony, the place where I spent the most time had roughly 110 boys. It was mostly runaways and delinquent kids. That was month after month of hell; I hated it. It's supposed to be a temporary emergency facility for kids who are abused, but it's more like a prison for children. You were always looking at big huge walls.

They had a behavior modification kind of program. Like, I could get a day pass or a weekend pass if I spent an afternoon playing football. They knew I was gay and that was the lifestyle I wanted, but they thought maybe they could change me. They had this deceiving slogan — "We'll help the adolescent with whatever problems they have and with whatever lifestyle they choose to live." But then all of a sudden, when they've got you in their grip, they try to brainwash you.

I had to see a therapist twice a week and he'd ask why I didn't like girls and tell me, you should try dating. It was all a big joke. I hadn't really been experimenting much sexually by then. I hadn't had a boyfriend. But I knew what I wanted. Mostly I kept my mouth shut, though, because I knew I'd get out of there eventually. It wasn't easy.

I was also in high school at the time and there were all sorts of rumors about me, innuendo, and comments, that went through campus. It's not easy for a kid in high school to be dealing with that. I didn't know any other kids who were gay. I thought I was one of the only people that had more than just the feelings. I might mentally have been blowing it out of proportion, but who knows what's real and what's in the mind in high school. I just know it was hell for me.

One day I took a lot of Valium and went to school. It was a stupid suicide attempt, but it was all because I was suffering from "What's this all about?" and "I need someone to talk to." The second time I took these antihistamines and they had to carry me away from school in an ambulance. It was real stupid, now that I look back on it.

When I first went to live with Tony, I didn't know he was gay. I had ideas but I didn't know for sure because it was a long time before he said, "I am gay." But there was something about him that I admired. He was always trying to help me. He got a psychologist for me. He gave me a lot of literature and books to read [about homosexuality]. And he always had answers to questions I had about being gay. He never tried to influence me, but he was the person who could say, "I want you to know I know what you're going through."

Such stories as Tim's suggest that agencies charged with the care of foster children may find it useful to consider the sexual orientation not just of foster parents but of foster children themselves. In several recent publications on homeless adolescents, "multiple placement youth," adolescents in unstable foster care, and disrupted older-child adoptions, however, the authors completely ignore the importance of sexual identity issues in considering why some children and youth experience ongoing disruptions in foster placements.[224]

For many lesbian, gay, bisexual, and "questioning" youth, their experience "on their own" or on the street, their distrust of adults, and the trauma associated with multiple, unsuccessful placements frequently combine with sexual identity issues to create serious emotional and adjustment problems. When it comes to assessing trauma, the harm done to these youth in anti-gay heterosexual homes cannot be calculated.

A List of Resources

A number of organizations exist whose work may be helpful to agencies considering issues related to lesbian and gay foster parents and child-placement policies. For the most part, these organizations make information available to the public either without charge or at low cost.

Organizations experienced in legal issues related to lesbian and gay parenting, including foster care and adoption, and in public policy formation; also skilled in strategies and techniques for dealing with media

National Center for Lesbian Rights
Adoption & Foster Parenting Project
1663 Mission Street, 5th Floor
San Francisco, CA 94103
415/621-0674   3 9 2 - 6 2 5 7

[Expert resource; sample briefs, in-service trainings for social service professionals and family court personnel]

---

[224] See, e.g., Barth, R., Berry, M., Carson, M. L., Goodfield, R. & Feinberg, B. (1986). Contributors to disruption and dissolution of older-child adoptions. *Child Welfare, 65*(4), 359-371; National Network of Runaway and Youth Services, Inc. (1985). *To whom do they belong? A profile of America's runaway and homeless youth and the programs that help them.* Washington, D.C.: Author; Pardeck, J. T. (1985). A profile of the child likely to experience unstable foster care. *Adolescence, 20*(79), 689-696; and Taber, M. & Proch, K. (1987). Placement stability for adolescents in foster care: Findings from a program experiment. *Child Welfare, 66*(5), 433-445.

Gay & Lesbian Advocates and Defenders
Post Office Box 218
Boston, MA 02112
617/426-3594

National Gay and Lesbian Task Force
Family Issues Project
1517 "U" Street NW
Washington, DC 20009
202/332-6483

Lambda Legal Defense and Education Fund
666 Broadway   *Susan Goldberg*
New York, NY 10012
212/995-8585

Organizations for lesbian and gay parents and their children; alternative family resources

CenterKids
The Family Project
Lesbian/Gay Community Services Center
208 West 13th Street
New York, NY 10011
212/620-7310

[Events and information for lesbian and gay parents. Resource
development and networking regarding parenting strategies.
Also support groups for children raised in alternative families.
Publishes *Kids' Talk* newsletter.]

National Gay and Lesbian Parents Coalition
Post Office Box 50360
Washington, DC 20004
202/583-8029

[National and regional conferences. Publishes *Just For Us*, a
newsletter by children for children raised in lesbian and gay
families (available c/o Post Office Box 644, Scarsdale, NY 10583).]

Lesbian and Gay Parenting Project
c/o Lyon-Martin Clinic
2480 Mission Street, Ste. 214
San Francisco, CA 94110
415/525-7312 or 415/641-0220

[Ongoing research projects regarding children of lesbian and gay
families; forums, workshops, speakers' bureau, and trainings.]

*Organizations experienced in evaluating and working with lesbian and
gay foster and adoptive parents*

The Triangle Project
c/o Gay & Lesbian Adolescent Social Services (GLASS)
8234 Santa Monica Boulevard, #214
West Hollywood, CA 90049
213/656-5005

[Recruitment and training of lesbian and gay foster parents for
children and youth.]

Aid to Adoption of Special Kids (AASK/America)
450 Sansome Street, Ste. 210
San Francisco, CA 94111
415/781-4112

Lutheran Social Services
1201 Payne Avenue
St. Paul, MN 55101
612/774-9507

*Organizations providing general social services to lesbian and gay youth;
potential foster care resources*[225]

Hetrick-Martin Institute/Harvey Milk High School
110 E. 23rd St., 10th Floor
New York, NY 10010
212/473-1113

Lavender Youth Recreation and Information Center (LYRIC)
c/o Operation Concern
1853 Market Street
San Francisco, CA 94103
415/531-4612 or 415/626-7000

Sexual Minority Youth Assistance League (SMILE)
1638 "R" Street NW
Washington, D.C. 20009
202/232-7506

The Shelter/Orion House
1020 Virginia Street
Seattle, WA 98101
206/622-3187

---

[225]   See also GLASS, listed above.

APPENDICES

Alternative Religious Approaches
To Homosexuality: A Bibliography

Bailey, D. S. (1975). *Homosexuality and the Western Christian tradition.* Hamden, CT: Archon Books. (Original work published 1955)

Balka, C. & Rose, A. (Eds.) (1989). *Twice blessed: On being lesbian, gay, and Jewish.* Boston, MA: Beacon Press.

Baum, G. (1974, 15 February). Catholic homosexuals. *Commonweal,* 479-482.

Boswell, J. (1980). *Christianity, social tolerance, and homosexuality.* Chicago: University of Chicago Press.

Clark, J. M., Brown, J. C. & Hochstein, L. M. (1990). Institutional religion and gay/lesbian oppression. *Marriage and Family Review,* 14(3/4), 265-284.

Commission on Social Justice (1982, July). *Homosexuality and social justice: Report of the Task Force on Gay/Lesbian issues.* San Francisco, CA: Archdiocese of San Francisco.

Comstock, G. D. (1987). Aliens in the promised land? *Union Seminary Quarterly Review,* 41(3-4), 93-104.

Cook, A. T. (1988). *And God loves each one: A resource for dialogue about the church and homosexuality.* Washington, D.C.: Dumbarton United Methodist Church. (Available from Dumbarton United Methodist Church, 3133 Dumbarton Street N.W., Washington, D.C. 20007)

Edwards, G. R. (1984). *Gay/Lesbian liberation: A biblical perspective.* NY: The Pilgrim's Press.

Gearhart, S. & Johnson, W. R. (1974). *Loving women/loving men: Gay liberation and the church.* San Francisco, CA: Glide Publications.

Gordis, R. (1978). *Love and sex: A modern Jewish perspective*. NY: Farrar, Strauss, & Giroux.

Gramick, J. & Fusey, P. (Eds.) (1988). *The Vatican and homosexuality: Reactions to the "Letter to the Bishops of the Catholic Church on the pastoral care of homosexual persons."* NY: Crossroad.

Horner, T. (1978). *Jonathan loved David: Homosexuality in biblical times*. Philadelphia: The Westminster Press.

Leopold, K. & Orians, T. (1985). *Theological pastoral resources: A collection of articles on homosexuality from a pastoral perspective*. Washington, D.C.: Dignity. (Original work published 1981) (Available from 1500 Massachusetts Avenue N.W., Washington, D.C. 20005)

Matt, H. J. (1978). Sin, crime, sickness or alternative life-style? A Jewish approach to homosexuality. *Judaism, 27*, 13-24.

McNaught, B. (1979). Gay and Catholic. In B. Berzon & R. Leighton (Eds.), *Positively gay*. Millbrae, CA: Celestial Arts.

McNeill, J. J. (1976). *The Church and the homosexual*. Kansas City, MO: Sheed Andrews and McMeel, Inc.

McNeill, J. J. (1988). *Taking a chance on God: Liberation theology for gays, lesbians, and their lovers, families, and friends*. Boston, MA: Beacon Press.

Nugent, R. (Ed.) (1983). *A challenge to love: Gay and lesbian Catholics in the Church*. NY: Crossroad Publishing Co.

Pennington, Rev. S. (1982). *But Lord, they're gay: A Christian pilgrimage*. Hawthorne, CA: Lambda Christian Fellowship. (Available from Post Office Box 1967, Hawthorne, CA 90205)

Scanzoni, L. & Mollenkott, V. R. (1980). *Is the homosexual my neighbor? Another Christian view*. San Francisco, CA: Harper & Row. (Original work published 1978)

Sherwood, Z. O. (1987). *Kairos: Confessions of a gay priest*. Boston: Alyson Publications.

Spero, M. H. (1979). Homosexuality: Clinical and ethical challenges. *Tradition, 17*(4), 53-73.

Topper, C. J. (1986). Spirituality as a component in counseling lesbian-gays. *Journal of Pastoral Counseling, 21*(1), 55-59.

Bibliography of Materials Related to Lesbian/Gay Parenting

Baptiste, D. A. (1987). The gay and lesbian stepparent family. In F. W. Bozett (Ed.), *Gay and lesbian parents* (pp. 112-137). New York: Praeger Press.

Baptiste, D. A. (1982). Issues and guidelines in the treatment of gay stepfamilies. In A. S. Gurman (Ed.), *Questions and answers in the practice of family therapy* (Vol II, pp. 112-137). New York: Brunner/Mazel.

Baptiste, D. (1987). Psychotherapy with gay and lesbian couples and their children in "stepfamilies": A challenge for marriage and family therapists. *Journal of Homosexuality, 14*(1/2), 223-238.

Bigner, J. J. & Jacobsen, R. B. (1989). The value of children to gay and heterosexual fathers. *Journal of Homosexuality, 18*(1/2), 163-172.

Bigner, J. J. & Bozett, F. W. (1990). Parenting by gay fathers. *Marriage and Family Review, 14*(3/4), 155-176.

Bigner, J. J. & Jacobsen, R. B. (1989). Parenting behaviors of homosexual and heterosexual fathers. *Journal of Homosexuality, 18*(1/2), 173-186.

Bozett, F. W. & Sussman, M. B. (1990). *Homosexuality and family relations.* Special issue of *Marriage and Family Review, 14*(3/4).

Bozett, F. W. (1988). Gay fatherhood. In P. Bronstein & C. P. Cowan (Eds.), *Fatherhood today: Men's changing role in the family* (pp. 214-235). New York: John Wiley & Sons.

Bozett, F. W. (Ed.) (1987). *Gay and lesbian parents.* New York: Praeger Press.

Bozett, F. W. (1980). Gay fathers: How and why they disclose their homosexuality to their children. *Family Relations, 29*(2), 173-179.

Bozett, F. W. (Ed.). (1989). Homosexuality and the Family. Special issue of the *Journal of Homosexuality, 18*(1/2).

Bozett, F. W. (1988). Social control of identity by children of gay fathers. *Western Journal of Nursing Research, 10*(5), 550-565.

Bozett, F. W. (1989). Gay fathers: A review of the literature. *Journal of Homosexuality, 18*(1/2), 137-162.

Bozett, F. W. (1985). Gay men as fathers. In S. Hanson & F. W. Bozett (Eds.), *Dimensions of fatherhood* (pp. 327-352). Beverly Hills, CA: Sage.

Bozett, F. W. (1981). Fathers who are homosexual. In L. Gross (Ed.), *The parents' guide to teenagers* (pp. 226-227). New York: MacMillan.

Cramer, D. (1986). Gay parents and their children: A review of research and practical implications. *Journal of Counseling and Development, 64*, 504-507.

DiLapi, E. M. (1989). Lesbian mothers and the motherhood hierarchy. *Journal of Homosexuality, 18*(1/2), 101-121.

Dunne, E. J. (1988). Helping gay fathers come out to their children. *Journal of Homosexuality, 14*(1/2), 213-222.

Fishel, A. H. (1983). Gay parents. *Issues in the Health Care of Women, 4*, 139-164.

Gantz, J. (1983). *Whose child cries: Children of gay parents talk about their lives.* Rolling Hills Estates, CA: Jalmar Press.

Golombok, S., Spencer, A. & Rutter, M. (1983). Children in lesbian and single-parent households: Psychosexual and psychiatric appraisal. *Journal of Child Psychology and Psychiatry, 24*(4), 551-572.

Goodman, B. (1980). Some mothers are lesbians. In E. Norman & A. Mancuso (Eds.), *Women's issues in social work practice* (pp. 153-180). Itasca, IL: F. E. Peacock Publishers.

Goodman, B. (1973). The lesbian mother. *American Journal of Orthopsychiatry, 43,* 283-284.

Gottman, J. S. (1990). Children of gay and lesbian parents. *Marriage and Family Review, 14*(3/4), 177-196.

Green, G. D. (1987). Lesbian mothers: Mental health considerations. In F. W. Bozett (Ed.), *Gay and lesbian parents* (pp. 188-198). New York: Praeger Press.

Green, R. (1978). Children of homosexuals seem headed straight. *Psychology Today, 12,* 44-46.

Green, R. (1978). Sexual identity of 37 children raised by homosexual or transsexual parents. *American Journal of Psychiatry, 135,* 692-697.

Green, R. (1985). Gender identity in childhood and later sexual orientation: Follow-up of 78 males. *American Journal of Psychiatry, 142,* 339-341.

Green, R. The best interests of the child with a lesbian mother. *Bulletin of the American Academy of Psychiatry and Law, 10*(1), 7-15.

Green, R., Mandel, J.B., Hotvedt, M.E., Gray, J. and Smith, L. (1986). Lesbian mothers and their children: A comparison with solo parent heterosexual mothers and their children. *Archives of Sexual Behavior, 15* (2), 167-184.

Harris, M. B. & Turner, P. H. (1985/86). Gay and lesbian parents. *Journal of Homosexuality, 12*(2), 101-113.

Hitchens, D. J. & Price, B. (1978/1979). Trial strategy in lesbian mother custody cases: The use of expert testimony. *Golden Gate Law Review, 9*(2), 451-479.

Hoeffer, B. (1981). Children's acquisition of sex-role behavior in lesbian-mother families. *American Journal of Orthopsychiatry, 51,* 536-544.

Hotvedt, M.E. & Mandel, J.B. (1982). Children of lesbian mothers. In W. Paul, J. D. Weinrich, J. C. Gonsiorek & M. E. Hotvedt (Eds.), *Homosexuality: Social, psychological, and biological issues* (pp. 275-285). Beverly Hills, CA: Sage.

Huggins, S. L. (1989). A comparative study of self-esteem of adolescent children of divorced lesbian mothers and divorced heterosexual mothers. *Journal of Homosexuality, 18*(1/2), 123-135.

Hunter, N. D. & Polikoff, N. D. (1976). Custody rights of lesbian mothers: Legal theory and litigation strategy. *Buffalo Law Review, 25*, 691-733.

Javaid, G. (1983). Case report: The sexual development of the adolescent daughter of a homosexual mother. *Journal of the American Academy of Child Psychiatry, 22*, 196-201.

Keating, B. R. & Brigman, K. M. L. (1986). Baseline information about homosexual fathers. *Sociology and Social Research, 70*(4), 287-289.

Kirkpatrick, M., Smith, K. & Roy, D. (1981). Lesbian mothers and their children: A comparative survey. *American Journal of Orthopsychiatry, 51*, 545-551.

Kirkpatrick, M. & Hitchens, D. J. (1985). Lesbian mothers/gay fathers. In P. Benedek & D. Shetky (Eds.), *Emerging issues in child psychiatry and the law* (pp. 108-119). New York: Brunner/Mazel.

Kirkpatrick, M. (1987). Clinical implications of lesbian mother studies. *Journal of Homosexuality, 14*(1/2), 201-211.

Kirkpatrick, M., Roy, R. & Smith, K. (1976). A new look at lesbian mothers. *Human Behavior, 5*, 60-61.

Kleber, D., Howell, R. & Tibbits-Kleber, A. (1986). The impact of parental homosexuality in child custody cases: A review of the literature. *Bulletin of the American Academy of Psychiatry and Law, 14*(1), 81-87.

Krestan, J. (1987). Lesbian daughters and lesbian mothers: The crisis of disclosure from a family systems perspective. *Journal of Psychotherapy and the Family, 3*(4), 113-30.

Kweskin, S. L. & Cook, A. S. (1982). Heterosexual and homosexual mothers' self-described sex-role behavior and ideal sex-role behavior in children. *Sex Roles, 8*(9), 967-975.

Lewin, E. & Lyons, T. A. (1982). Everything in its place: The coexistence of lesbianism and motherhood. In W. Paul, J. D. Weinrich, J. C. Gonsiorek, & M. E. Hotvedt (Eds.), *Homosexuality: Social, psychological, and biological issues* (pp. 249-273). Beverly Hills, CA: Sage.

Lewin E. (1981). Lesbianism and motherhood: Implications for child custody. *Human Organizations, 40,* 6-14.

Lewis, K. G. (1980). Children of lesbian parents: Their point of view. *Social Work, 25*(3), 198-203.

Maddox, B. (1982). Homosexual parents. *Psychology Today, 16*(2), 62-69.

McGuire, M. & Alexander, N. (1985). Artificial insemination of single women. *Fertility and Sterility, 43*(2), 182-184.

Miller, B. (1979). Gay fathers and their children. *Family Coordinator, 28,* 544-552.

Miller, B. (1979). Unpromised paternity: the life-styles of gay fathers. In M. Levine (Ed.), *Gay men* (pp. 239-252). New York: Harper & Row.

Morin, S. F. & Schultz, S. J. (1978). The gay movement and the rights of children. *Journal of Social Issues, 34*(2), 137-147.

Mucklow, B. & Phelan, K. (1979). Lesbian and traditional mothers' responses to adult response to child behavior and self-concept. *Psychological Reports, 44,* 880-882.

Nungesser, L. G. (1980). Theoretical bases for research on the acquisition of sex-roles by children of lesbian mothers. *Journal of Homosexuality, 5*(3), 177-187.

Osman, S. (1972). My stepfather is a she. *Family Process, 11,* 209-218.

Pagelow, M. (1980). Heterosexual and lesbian single mothers: A comparison of problems, coping and solutions. *Journal of Homosexuality, 5,* 189-204.

Pennington, S. B. (1987). Children of lesbian mothers. In F. W. Bozett (Ed.), *Gay and lesbian parents* (pp. 58-74). New York: Praeger Press.

Polikoff, N. (1986). Lesbian mothers, lesbian families: Legal obstacles, legal challenges. *Review of Law and Social Change, 14*(4), 907-914.

Rees, R. A. (1979). A comparison of children of lesbian and single heterosexual mothers on three measures of socialization. (Doctoral dissertation, California School of Professional Psychology, Berkeley, 1979). *Dissertation Abstracts International*, 40, 3418-3419B.

Ricketts, W. & Achtenberg, R. (1990). Adoption and foster parenting for lesbians and gay men: Creating new traditions in family. *Marriage and Family Review, 14*(3/4), 83-118.

Ricketts, W. & Achtenberg, R. A. (1987). The adoptive and foster gay and lesbian parent. In F. W. Bozett (Ed.), *Gay and lesbian parents* (pp. 89-111). New York: Praeger Press.

Riddle, D. & Arguelles, M. (1981). Children of gay parents: Homophobia's victims. In I. Stuart & L. Abt (Eds.), *Children of separation and divorce: Management and treatment* (pp. 174-197). New York: Van Nostrand Reinhold.

Riddle, D. I. (1978). Relating to children: Gays as role models. *Journal of Social Issues, 34*, 38-58.

Robinson, B. & Skeen, P. (1982). Sex-role orientation of gay fathers versus gay non-fathers. *Perceptual and Motor Skills, 55*, 1055-1059.

Robinson, B. E. & Barrett, R. L. (1986). Gay fathers. In B. E. Robinson & R. L. Barrett (Eds.), *The developing father: Emerging roles in contemporary society* (pp. 145-168). New York: Guilford Press.

Ross, J. L. (1988). Challenging boundaries: An adolescent in a homosexual family. *Journal of Family Psychology, 2*(2), 227-240.

Russotto, J. (1980). Children of homosexual parents. In *The many dimensions of family practice: Proceedings of the North American Symposium on Family Practice* (pp. 112-120). New York: Family Service Association of America.

Scanzoni, L. D. & Scanzoni, J. (1981). Gay parenthood and marriage. In L. D. Scanzoni & J. Scanzoni (Eds.), *Men, women, and change* (pp. 235-261). New York: McGraw Hill.

Shulenburg, J. (1985). *Gay parenting.* New York: Anchor Press/ Doubleday.

Skeen, P. & Robinson, B. (1985). Gay fathers and nongay fathers. Relationships with their parents. *Journal of Sex Research, 21,* 86-91.

Skeen, P. & Robinson, B. (1984). Family background of gay fathers: A descriptive study. *Psychological Reports, 54,* 999-1005.

Steckel, A. (1987). Psychosocial development of children of lesbian mothers. In F. W. Bozett (Ed.), *Gay and lesbian parents* (pp. 75-85). New York: Praeger Press.

Voeller, B. & Walters, J. (1978). Gay fathers. *Family Coordinator, 27,* 149-157.

Weeks, R. Derdeyn, A. & Langman, M. (1975). Two cases of children of homosexuals. *Child Psychiatry and Human Development, 6,* 26-32.

Whittlin, W. (1983). Homosexuality and child custody: A psychiatric viewpoint. *Conciliation Courts Review, 21*(1), 77-79.

Wismont, J. M. & Reame, N. E. (1989). The lesbian childbearing experience: Assessing developmental tasks. *Image: Journal of Nursing Scholarship, 21*(3), 137-141.

Wyers, N. L. (1987). Homosexuality in the family: Lesbian and gay spouses. *Social Work, 32*(2), 143-148.

Professional Policy Statements

Statement of the National Association of Social Workers

Lesbian and Gay Issues

Background

The oppression of gay men and lesbians has taken form in religion, culture, law, and social sanction. American society, strongly influenced by interpretations of Judeo-Christian moral codes, traditionally has condemned homosexuality. This theological interpretation has led to the exclusion of lesbians and gay men from participation in religious services. Other results include legal and institutional discrimination as well as violence against lesbians and gay men.

Recently, religious groups have begun to reexamine their historical positions of discrimination and disapproval. Although many religious denominations have issued working documents calling for a reexamination of theological concepts in reference to human sexuality and lesbians and gay men have organized within their respective churches and synagogues to foster positive change, to date, most lesbians and gay men still are denied positive affirmation and unqualified acceptance within their religious institutions.

Moral codes also have shaped the legal system, which criminalized many acts of sexual expression. In most states, sodomy laws make sexual expression a crime for gay men. Legal rights are denied lesbians and gay men in other ways as well:

- Same-sex couples do not have the right to marry.

- Lesbians and gay men have been denied custody of their children, as well as the right to provide foster and adoptive care.

◆ Their partners do not have the same rights of inheritance and decision making as biological next of kin.

◆ Employment rights, housing, access to resources and services, and the rights to immigration and naturalization routinely are denied to lesbians and gay men.

◆ Lesbians and gay men are excluded from military service or are dishonorably dismissed if their sexual orientation is known.

In addition, violence against lesbians and gay men has been documented by public authorities and advocacy groups. Anti-gay violence and discrimination against lesbians and gay men have increased significantly as a result of the acquired immune deficiency syndrome (AIDS) epidemic.

The Kinsey studies in 1948 documented clearly the broad variation of human sexual behavior and the prevalence of homosexuality in the American population[1] Kinsey estimated that lesbians and gay men comprise approximately 10 percent of the U.S. population. At least 20 million lesbians and gay men endure lack of access to social, physical, and emotional resources; discrimination; and stigmatization as criminal, deviant, and pathological.

Statement of Issues

As helping professionals, social workers are guided by the *Code of Ethics*, which has been adopted by the Delegate Assembly of the National Association of Social Workers (NASW)[2] Relative to the social worker's ethical responsibility to clients, the *Code of Ethics* states:

> The social workers should not practice, condone, facilitate or collaborate with any form of discrimination on the basis of race, color, sex, sexual orientation, age, religion, national origin, marital status, political belief, mental or physical handicap, or any other preference or personal characteristic, condition or status.

Relative to the social worker's ethical responsibility to society, the *Code of Ethics* further states,

> The social worker should act to prevent and elimi-
> nate discrimination against any person or group on
> the basis of race, color, sex, sexual orientation, age,
> religion, national origin, marital status, political
> belief, mental or physical handicap, or any prefer-
> ence or personal characteristic, condition or status.

> The social worker should act to ensure that all
> persons have access to the resources, services and
> opportunities which they require.

> The social worker should act to expand choice and
> opportunity for all persons, with special regard to
> disadvantaged or oppressed groups and persons.

Because the social work profession has a responsibility for serving disadvantaged or oppressed groups and persons, social workers must ascertain the needs and promote the well-being of lesbians and gay men. A percentage of social workers and their clients are members of this minority group.

Despite the values and ethics prescribed by the social work profession, individual social workers are not immune to cultural attitudes and values that are antithetical to those of the social work profession. Homophobia, the irrational fear and hatred of those who are sexually oriented toward persons of the same sex, has given and continues to give rise to a host of discriminatory practices both institutionally and individually in American soci-ety. Lesbian and gay individuals, therefore, frequently experience the same kind of supremacist prejudice that figures in racism, sexism, ageism, classism, and anti-Semitism. Prejudice toward and discomfort with lesbians and gay men or their behavior renders social work practice with such clients ineffective and frequently damaging. Social workers must examine their attitudes and feelings to ensure that they are not having a negative impact on their clients.

Lesbians and gay male social workers are employed in all areas of social work practice. Many still experience prejudice and discrimination in their professional lives, or would if they openly acknowledged their sexual orientation. The necessity for lesbians and gay men to remain totally or even partially "closeted" in their professional lives is irrational and potentially damaging to the development of their highest potential. Consequently, social workers must create an atmosphere that is open to and accepting of their lesbian and gay male colleagues.

At various times, mental health professionals, including social workers, have described such sexual behaviors as masturbation, sexual relations between single persons, pregnancy in unmarried women, and birth control as pathological. Yet it behooves professionals who hold such ideas to modify their approaches as new information and views of behavior become prevalent. Toward this end, both the American Psychiatric Association and the American Psychological Association progressively have reexamined homosexuality in the past two decades. They no longer define it as a mental disorder. The social work profession has done the same and continues that process through the updating of this policy statement.

Policy Statement

NASW recognizes that homosexuality has existed throughout history (as has heterosexuality) and that same-sex orientation should be afforded the same respect as that of opposite-sex sexual orientation. NASW asserts that discrimination and prejudice directed against any minority group is damaging to the mental health not only of the affected minority but of the society as a whole. NASW is committed to work toward the building of a society in which all people will be accepted as equals without regard to their sexual orientation. NASW affirms that lesbian and gay individuals are entitled to the rights of self-determination, self-definition, and self-expression, as long as the rights of others are not infringed.

To this end, NASW shall support legislation, regulation, policies, judicial review, political action, demonstrations, and other appropriate means that will establish and protect equal rights for all persons without regard to their sexual orientation. This includes, but by no means is limited to, working for the adoption of policies and legislation to end all forms of discrimination against lesbians and gay men at the federal, state, and local levels in all institutions, including churches and synagogues, and in both the public and private sectors. NASW will support the repeal of all laws against any forms of consensual adult sexual activity as well. NASW will work toward the elimination of prejudice, both inside and outside the profession.

Homophobia and its resultant discrimination give rise to "internalized oppression." This creates problems regarding self-esteem and self-image for lesbians and gay men. Social workers need to be aware of this when working with lesbians and gay men.

NASW should develop and sponsor educational programs designed to train social workers in the area of human sexuality, including homosexuality and the needs of the lesbian and gay communities. In cooperation with the Council on Social Work Education (CSWE), NASW would encourage instructors of social work educational programs to include lesbian and gay issues in their curricula. NASW, in cooperation with CSWE, should encourage social work educational institutions to develop nondiscrimination policies regarding lesbian and gay male students and staff. In cooperation with CSWE and other institutions, NASW should undertake research into all areas related to homosexuality and practice and policy development.

Notes and References

1. A. F. Kinsey, W. B. Pomeroy, and C. E. Martins, *Sexual Behavior in the Human Male* (Philadelphia: W. B. Saunders Co., 1948).

2. National Association of Social Workers, *Code of Ethics of the National Association of Social Workers* (Silver Spring, MD.: National Association of Social Workers, Inc., 1980).

◆ Policy statement approved by the NASW Delegate Assembly, November 1987. This statement supersedes the policy state ment on gay issues approved by the Delegate Assembly in 1977.

For further information, contact the National Association of Social Workers, Inc., 7981 Eastern Avenue, Silver Spring, MD 20910. Telephone: 301-565-0333 or 800- 638-8799.

Statement of the National Association of Social Workers

FOSTER CARE AND ADOPTION

Background

Foster care and adoption have long served as society's way of providing alternative care to children who — on either a temporary or permanent basis and for a variety of reasons — cannot live with their families of origin. Although these services have provided needed assistance for many children, both have been subject to problems that have limited their potential for meeting children's needs.

During the past 10 years, the social service systems that provide alternative care to children have changed significantly. With the passage of P.L. 96-272 in 1980, state child welfare agencies were encouraged and, in some areas, mandated to improve their foster care and adoption programs. Since that year, the population of children in foster care diminished for a period of time. The decrease resulted in part from a new emphasis on services that prevents removal of children from their homes and on carefully planned case review systems. Still, many children enter foster care or remain in foster care because of a lack of resources and prevention services in their communities.

In addition, the foster care and adoption populations have changed. There is an increase in the proportion of hard-to-place and special needs children such as children who have the following characteristics: minority; older; developmentally disabled; medically needy; acquired immune deficiency syndrome (AIDS), AIDS-related complex (ARC), and human immunodeficiency virus (HIV) positive; or emotionally disturbed.

The social work profession — considering the major role the profession plays in the development and delivery of foster care and adoption — has a responsibility to assist in assessing public social policy and practice with regard to such services. Social workers should ensure that the services reflect the best and most current knowledge in the field to meet consistently the needs of children and of the community. Social workers who participate in foster care and adoption policy development and in service delivery must be knowledgeable about national standards in foster care and adoption and also must uphold professional practice standards.

Statement of Issues

Recognition must be given to children's needs for security, continuity of parenting relationships, and nurturing in foster care and adoption services systems. In addition, families must be strengthened and supported as the primary and preferred source for meeting children's physical and psychological needs. Therefore, societal intervention into the parent-child relationship must be considered very carefully so that such intervention meets the child's interest both immediately and over time. The child's enduring ties to a family must be recognized. Child welfare practice cannot be separated from a family systems approach.

Appropriate and adequate information regarding resources, rights, and responsibilities must be available to all parties in foster care and adoption proceedings. Specifically, society's responsibility for ensuring comprehensive quality services, with particular attention to the special needs of high-risk children and the resources necessary to meet those needs, much be recognized. Also, the adoptee's right to know about his or her birth parents and the limits of confidentiality must be addressed for all parties.

An emerging and growing population of children in need of services are children with AIDS or ARC and the children who test HIV positive. The complex interplay of social and medical factors implicit in the care of these children presents particular challenges in foster care and adoption and requires a renewed commitment to assure children with AIDS-related conditions the same opportunities to have permanent families as other children, without isolation and segregation.

Comprehensive quality services are of particular concern in the provision of service to children with AIDS-related conditions. All services provided this special population must be grounded in a multidisciplinary approach and include well thought out medical treatment where needed.

Research, training, and evaluation of foster care and adoption delivery systems and services must be funded and disseminated. A national information system is essential for providing information for policy development and resource allocations.

Policy Statement

An adequate foster care and adoption policy designed to provide the best care for all children in need of such services should be predicatèd on four fundamental principles:

1. Every child has the right to a permanent, continuous, and nurturing relationship with a parenting person or persons who convey to the child an enduring sense of love and care. The child should perceive himself or herself as a valued family member. This right shall supersede the right of birth parents to maintain legal custody when such custody is physically or emotionally harmful.

2. The opportunity to provide such a nurturing environment is the primary responsibility of the child's family. It thus becomes society's primary responsibility to provide the necessary services and supports required to safeguard and enhance, with every available means, the ability of all families to fulfill this essential role. Failing this, it become society's responsibility to provide for expeditious, alternative arrangements that are permanent and meet the child's physical, mental, and emotional needs.

3. Societal intervention into the parent-child relationship is an extremely serious action, which should be pursued only when the child's right to a safe, secure, and nurturing home is seriously threatened. Services should be provided with sensitivity, professional skill, regard for the legal rights of the parties involved, and a sense of the limitations and potential outcomes of such an intervention.

4. Policy and budget leaders need adequate data through a national information system for the purpose of policy development and resource allocation.

The four basic principles undergird an entire approach to foster care and adoption. The following policy statement includes generic principles that apply to both foster care and adoption as well as principles specifically related to foster care and adoption, respectively.

Generic child placement principles include the following:

♦ Both foster care and adoption services should be built on and used within an adequately financed family service system. The National Association of Social Workers (NASW) has recognized the need for such a comprehensive approach, as well as the right of persons to employment opportunities or income supports or both that enable them to meet basic family needs.

♦ The objective of every child's placement should be to provide a safe, nurturing, and secure alternative home when it is not possible for the child to remain with his or her family.

♦ Placement decisions should reflect a child's need for continuity — safeguarding both the child's right to consistent care and to service arrangements. Agencies must recognize each child's need to retain significant engagement with his or her parents and extended family and respect the integrity of each child's ethnicity and cultural heritage.

◆ Termination of parental rights, whether voluntary or involuntary, should never be undertaken lightly. Adequate information should be provided, along with full exploration of the alternatives and due process.

◆ Persons involved with the foster care system, adoption proceedings, or child and family services have the right to receive adequate information — from the appropriate agency, court, or community sources — especially regarding their rights, prerogatives, and responsibilities, and adequate legal representation.

◆ Ongoing research and evaluation with input from clients should be used by service providers to form and guide policy and practices in foster care and adoption.

◆ A child's family should receive sufficient and timely support services to prevent the need for substitute care. Neither foster care nor adoption services should be used merely because they provide a convenient choice in a difficult situation.

◆ Decision makers in child placement services always should be sensitive to the inherent trauma resulting from removing a child from familiar surroundings and family members. The child's need for an improved environment must be balanced against the possible damage that could result from the separation. The decision makers also must explore alternatives to out-of-home placement and actualize the concept of "reasonable efforts to prevent removal from the home." The decision-making process must include at all times the development and implementation of a permanent plan for the child. This permanent plan can include a timely decision to terminate parental rights when it is clear that the child cannot remain in or return to his or her family. For some children, permanent planning would include preparation for independent living.

◆ All independently made arrangements for children should conform to and be judged by the same principles of care established throughout this policy and should conform to national standards of foster care and adoption practice.

◆ Agencies must ensure removal of any barriers that prevent children from being placed in permanent homes. Financial barriers can be breached by strong use and expansion of existing adoption subsidy programs. Barriers that are unsupported by tested experience, such as resistance to using single parents, foster parents (for adoption), and nontraditional family patterns including lesbian and gay parents as potential foster care and adoption resources, must be removed.

◆ Professional persons at various levels in the government must monitor aggressively and carefully foster care and adoption services — whether provided by the public or the voluntary sector. Professionals should have expertise in child welfare to ensure that caring, comprehensive, permanent planning and services for children are provided.

◆ Patterns of funding for foster care and adoption services should guarantee quality services to all children regardless of their race, language, capabilities, religion, geographic location, or socioeconomic status.

◆ Foster care and adoption agencies must be administered and staffed by trained social workers. Caseloads should never exceed the ability of workers to provide reasonable, full, and careful attention to each child and his or her family.

◆ The long-range advantage to society in providing quality family services — including but not limited to foster care and adoption — should be promoted. This means advancing the concept ofcommunity responsibility for all children's needs and seeking to improve the public image and understanding of foster care and adoption.

◆ The social work profession stresses the importance of ethnic and cultural sensitivity. An effort to maintain a child's identify and her or his ethnic heritage should prevail in all services and placement actions that involve children in foster care and adoption programs, including adherence to the principles articulated in the Indian Child Welfare Act.

Principles related to foster care include the following:

◆ Foster care of children should be viewed as a support service during critical periods in the life of the family after all alternatives to out-of-home placement have been explored and tried. Foster care should not be seen as a penalty for child neglect or inability to cope with the difficulties of raising children in a stressful world. Foster care should be viewed as a support that enables parents to resume parenting responsibilities.

◆ When foster care becomes the intervention of choice, services to reunify the child with her or his family should begin immediately. These services should work toward improving the conditions in the home and facilitating the child's return. Services should be limited by time and planned. When it is clear that progress is not being made to improve conditions, a permanent plan that provides the best alternative for the child should be implemented.

◆ Vigorous recruitment, mutual selection, initial and ongoing training of foster parents, as well as adequate financial support are seen as prerequisites to a successful foster care system. Foster parents need to be particularly sensitive to the special needs of children in their care and to be able to work with and support birth parents who are making appropriate efforts to ensure the return of their children.

◆ Comprehensive and specialized training of foster parents should be required a precondition to foster home licensure and inservice training should be required as a condition for continuing licensure.

◆ Foster parents should be viewed as partners in the service delivery team. Therefore, resources are needed to assist the foster parents in providing care to the child. Resources for foster families should include day care, respite care, peer support, counseling, and parent education.

◆ Liability insurance for foster parents should be the responsibility of the placing agencies.

◆ Full and prompt reimbursement of maintenance costs and fees for services provided by foster parents should be viewed as an essential part of the agency's plan of care for the child and an investment in both the child and society. The agency also should acknowledge that there are children with special needs regardless of age and establish a cost schedule accordingly.

◆ A variety of foster care arrangements should be available to the child welfare agency, including family foster care, group home care, therapeutic foster care, day treatment foster care, and institutional care, so that appropriate placements can be made for all children who need temporary, emergency, planned long-term, and specialized foster care. The spectrum of arrangements should include supervised independent living programs for those children who are making the transition from foster care to living on their own.

◆ Child welfare agencies should ensure that each child in foster care will have a case plan. The plan should include the reasons the child was removed from the home; the special needs of the child while in and out of home care; and the services to be provided to the parents, child, and foster parents. The plan will assist in reunifying the family, or if that is not feasible, will result in permanent placement. Case plans should be reviewed periodically by the agency and the court where mandated by law.

◆ The agency's periodic case review system should include all parties, including the caseworker and supervisor, the birth parents and other relatives of the child, foster parents, and the child (if of appropriate age). In addition, an objective party who is not involved in the management of the case or delivery of services may be involved in the review of the status of the child in care. Each party to the service planning process should be provided with a copy of the initial case plan and subsequent revised plans and agreements.

◆ Recruitment of foster parents from each relevant racial and ethnic group should be pursued vigorously to meet the needs of children who require placement. Placement of choice should be within the child's family of origin, among relatives who can provide a more stable environment for the child during the period of family crisis. If no such relatives are available, every effort should be made to place a child in the home of foster parents who are similar in racial and ethnic background to the child's own family.

◆ NASW will advocate policies that support systematic involvement of child welfare agencies with foster parents. Foster parents should be trained and compensated and receive continuous support commensurate with the skill level.

Principles related to adoption include the following:

◆ All parties to adoption are individuals whose needs
and rights should be respected and considered to
the greatest extent possible. Full recognition must
be given to a child's right to and need for birth
family ties and the right of those birth parents,
regardless of their condition, to the services they
may need to parent their child and prevent the
need for adoption. The child must, nevertheless,
be seen as the primary client whose need for a
permanent plan must take priority.

◆ Adoption policy and practice should recognize that
services should be extended to all parties involved
in the adoption and be made available for as long
as they are needed and desired. This includes
services, if needed, long beyond the legal consum-
mation of the adoption.

◆ Special attention should be given to children with
special needs (children who are older; physically,
intellectually, or emotionally handicapped;
members of sibling groups; and of minority backgrounds), to ensure protection of their right to a
caring environment. This care extends to recruitment of appropriate families and professional
services throughout the adoption process and
beyond legalization.

◆ Publicly funded subsidies should be available in all
cases in which the cost of the child's permanent
care becomes a barrier to appropriate adoptive
placement. Adoption subsidies must be available
to meet the child's special needs. Also, if adoption
subsidies are needed through the child's minority
and transition to adulthood, the subsidies must be
adequate.

◆ The provision of current, viable information to all parties involved in the adoption is the responsibility of the agency. The identifying nature of the information shared is based on the law or the agreement of the parties affected. No information is to be provided to anyone outside of those directly affected by the adoption (adopted person, birth family, and adoptive family). Care must be taken before sharing information about a person who previously has been assured confidentiality. Efforts should be made to get the consent of a person who had been assured confidentiality. Compelling professional reasons should allow for sharing of identifying information. The need and right of adoptees to know their birth origin should be recognized and respected. This right extends to requests from adult adoptees for identifying information. If a reunion is requested with a birth relative, the service providers should attempt to provide counseling and intermediary services, fully cognizant of the sensitivities of all the parties involved. Both adoptive parents and birth parents should be informed of the limits of confidentiality.

◆ The social work profession, along with social agencies, has a responsibility to advocate for appropriate changes in the law and the training of social workers, which would facilitate the sharing of identifying information between adult adoptees and birth parents when both parties are in agreement. When indicated, the adoptive parent should be involved in this process.

◆ Recruitment of and placement with adoptive parents from each relevant ethnic or racial group should be available to meet the needs of children.

◆ NASW opposes placements made by third parties who are not related to the child or who are not licensed as placement agencies. The reason is the need to protect the rights and ensure the welfare of children through careful preplacement selection and early monitoring of placements by qualified professionals. However, in states in which placements by third parties are legally recognized, NASW advocates that assessment and supervision of adoptive family and child be carried out by professionally trained social workers. In such states, NASW will continue to support appropriate legislation to eliminate third-party placement.

◆ Policy statement approved by the NASW Delegate Assembly, November 1987. This statement supersedes the policy statement on gay issues approved by the Delegate Assembly in 1977.

For further information, contact the National Association of Social Workers, Inc., 7981 Eastern Avenue, Silver Spring, MD 20910. Telephone: 301-565-0333 or 800-638-8799.

Statement of the American Psychiatric Association

Position Statement on Discrimination in Selection of Foster Parents

This statement was approved by the Assembly in May 1986 and by the Board of Trustees in June 1986.

Children do not choose to be foster children. Nonetheless, in the real world foster care is important and necessary. Numbers of foster children are increasing, and there are rarely enough foster families available to meet children's needs. Because good foster families often are unavailable, children are often neglected and/or placed in institutional facilities for extended periods of time when these may be developmentally damaging.

Foster placement is always a compromise. Consideration of foster placement requires flexibility, not rigidity. There is relatively little support for foster parents and for standards for good foster care. The main focus of assessment for foster placement must be on the adequacy of the foster parent(s)' caretaking capacity for a particular child at a particular time, considered in context with all realistic alternatives. Child psychiatrists and other child health professionals recognize that single factor criteria are simplistic and that a professional perspective mandates comprehensive multi-factor determination.

The American Psychiatric Association and its District Branches are available to suggest psychiatrists with a wide range of expertise and experience for consultation and development of constructive policies and criteria for foster parents. Additional input from other professionals in social work, psychology, and child development is also available.

The Council on Children, Adolescents and Their Families of the APA has reviewed the literature and a wide body of clinical experience. It is recognized that more research would be useful. However, the Council finds that the available research and experience show that single factors (e.g., being a single parent, homosexual, or elderly) should not necessarily or automatically rule out selection of a potential foster parent.

All potential foster parents should be evaluated, carefully and comprehensively, by experts using multiple factors regarding their suitability to meet the needs of their potential foster children at that time and in that setting.

Statement of the American Psychological Association

APA POLICY STATEMENTS ON LESBIAN AND GAY ISSUES

Discrimination Against Homosexuals

At its January 1975 meeting, Council [Ed. note: The Council of Representatives, the governing body of the American Psychological Association] adopted a statement of policy regarding homosexuals, recommended by BSERP [Ed. note: The Board of Social and Ethical Responsibility for Psychology, a Standing Board provided by the American Psychological Association's Bylaws] and amended by the Board of Directors and Council, and adapted from a statement adopted by the Association of Gay Psychologists Caucus Meeting in New Orleans in September 1974. Further, Council voted that the Association's Statement of Policy regarding Equal Employment Opportunity be amended to include *sexual orientation* among the prohibited discriminations listed in the statement. Following is the Policy Statement regarding Discrimination against Homosexuals:

1. The American Psychological Association supports the action taken on December 15, 1973, by the American Psychiatric Association, removing homosexuality from that Association's official list of mental disorders. The American Psychological Association therefore adopts the following resolution:

   Homosexuality per se implies no impairment in judgement, stability, reliability, or general social and vocational capabilities: Further, the American Psychological Association urges all mental health professionals to take the lead in removing the stigma of mental illness that has long been association with homosexual orientations.

2. Regarding discrimination against homosexuals, the American Psychological Association adopts the following resolution concerning their civil and legal rights.

    The American Psychological Association deplores all public and private discrimination in such areas as employment, housing, public accommodation, and licensing against those who engage in or have engaged in homosexual activities and declares that no burden of proof of such judgement, capacity, or reliability shall be placed upon these individuals greater than that imposed on any other persons. Further, the American Psychological Association supports and urges the enactment of civil rights legislation at the local, state and federal level that would offer citizens who engage in acts of homosexuality the same protections now guaranteed to others on the basis of race, creed, color, etc. Further, the American Psychological Association supports and urges the repeal of all discriminatory legislation singling out homosexual acts by consenting adults in private.
    (Conger, 1975, p. 655)

Child Custody or Placement

At its September 1976 meeting, the Council adopted the following resolution, initiated by the Task Force on the Status of Lesbian and Gay Psychologists of the Board of Social and Ethical Responsibility for Psychology (BSERP): "The sex, gender identity or sexual orientation of natural or prospective adoptive or foster parents should not be the sole or primary variable considered in custody or placement cases."
(Conger, 1977, p. 432)